MH00777208

SILVER
PRESS

SPACE CRONE

URSULA KROEBER LE GUIN (1929-2018) was a celebrated and
beloved author of twenty-one novels, eleven volumes of
short stories, four collections of essays, twelve children's
books, six volumes of poetry and four of translation. The
breadth and imagination of her work earned her six Nebu-
las, nine Hugos and SFWA's Grand Master, along with the
PEN/Malamud and many other awards. In 2014 she was
awarded the National Book Foundation Medal for Distinguished Contribution to American Letters, and in 2016
joined the short list of authors to be published in their
lifetimes by the Library of America.

ARWEN CURRY is the producer and director of the feature
documentary *Worlds of Ursula K. Le Guin* (2018), which was
nominated for a Hugo Award and broadcast nationally
on PBS American Masters. She also worked on *EAMES: The
Architect and The Painter*, *American Jerusalem: Jews and The Making of
San Francisco*, *Regarding Susan Sontag* and *KQED Science*. She is a
graduate of UC Berkeley Journalism School and a former
editor of the punk magazine *Maximum Rock'n'Roll*. She lives
in San Francisco.

SO MAYER is a writer and organiser. Their most recent book
is the essay *A Nazi Word for a Nazi Thing* (Peninsula, 2020).
Truth or Dare, a collection of speculative fiction, will be published by Cipher Press in summer 2023. They work with

queer feminist film curation collective Club des Femmes and independent bookstore Burley Fisher.

SARAH SHIN is a writer, publisher and curator whose work includes making books, texts, gardens, games, scents, spaces, portals and practices. She is a founder of Ignota, a creative publishing and curatorial house exploring consciousness, technology and healing; Silver Press, the feminist publisher; New Suns, a curatorial project that began as a literary festival at the Barbican Centre; and Standard Deviation, a spatial practice exploring the coincidence of psychic, geometric and inhabited space.

Space Crone

Ursula K. Le Guin

SILVER
PRESS

CONTENTS

INTRODUCTION

CHANGING HER MIND OR,
HOW THE SPACE CRONE BECAME

'**N**arrative,' according to Ursula K. Le Guin, 'is a stratagem of mortality. It is a means, a way of living.' For Le Guin, narrative – science fiction in particular – provided a carrier bag in which she carried new ways of living, capacious enough to embrace her wild diversity of themes, including anarchism, dreams, fantasy and gender.

Le Guin began a lifetime of shaping these themes in Berkeley, California, in the academic household of Theodora and Alfred Louis Kroeber. Born on 21 October 1929, Ursula was the youngest of four, and grew up with her three older brothers, Clifton, Theodore and Karl, in a household at once intensely bookish and open to the natural world.

Her father was an anthropologist and the first professor appointed to the Department of Anthropology at Berkeley, where he helped to establish the department's museum. His work on linguistic anthropology would later echo in Le Guin's worlds, for example as the power of naming that underlies the magic of the Earthsea books. He remains best known for his work with Indigenous people in California. Theodora wrote two popular books about their family friend Ishi, the last survivor of the Yahi people.

As Le Guin reflected in a talk at Berkeley's Department of Anthropology, in the building named after her father and then renamed in January 2021 to 'better support . . . the diversity of today's academic community', the work of early anthropologists is viewed more critically today. In 'Indian Uncles', she observes that novelists share with anthropologists 'the same moral problem, the problem of exploitation, but we rarely face it in so stark a form'. In the same essay, she describes the influential presence of Juan Dolores (Papago) and Robert Spott (Yurok), in the Kroeber household, offering the children a multiplicity of world-views. Summers were spent at the family ranch in Napa Valley, where Indigenous friends would share stories and legends. 'I didn't know anything,' Le Guin concludes her talk. 'I thought everybody spoke Yurok. But I knew where the centre of the world was.'

Le Guin grew up reading stories, myths and fairy tales from around the world, as well as Virginia Woolf and James Frazier. Much of her adolescence was spent working her way through the French section at the Berkeley Public Library, an encounter that would lead her to study Romance literature at university; global literatures, translation and poetry remained constants. In the introduction to her 1997 rendition of Lao Tzu's *Tao Te Ching*, Le Guin recalled her father's much-read edition of Paul Carus's 1898 translation, 'bound in yellow cloth stamped with blue and red Chinese designs and characters . . . I was lucky to discover [Lao Tzu] so young, so that I could live with his book my whole life long.'

This early exposure to ancient Chinese thought had a profound influence on Le Guin's writing, which often uses moments of cultural contact and exchange to suggest alternatives to the Western status quo. In the Tao, yin and yang describe sets of separate yet interrelated forces that appear dualistic but in fact form a harmonious whole – a symbolic language that allows for nuanced expressions of difference, with each containing the other. The common association of yin with the feminine and yang with the masculine should, particularly from a feminist perspective, be understood as speaking more of the dynamic relationship between polarities, rather than of essentialist natures. In Le Guin's radical lexicon, yang and yin become, among other things, expressions of a utopian dialectic:

> Utopia has been yang. In one way or another, from Plato on, utopia has been the big yang motorcycle trip. Bright, dry, clear, strong, firm, active, aggressive, lineal, progressive, creative, expanding, advancing and hot.
>
> Our civilisation is now so intensely yang that any imagination of bettering its injustices or eluding its self-destructiveness must involve a reversal . . . To attain the constant, we must return, go round, go inward, go yinward. What would a yin utopia be? It would be dark, wet, obscure, weak, yielding, passive, participatory, circular, cyclical, peaceful, nurturant, retreating, contracting, and cold.

Like her near-contemporary, the revolutionary philosopher and activist Grace Lee Boggs, Le Guin was committed to slow action in the service of long change. Her much-loved essay *The Carrier Bag Theory of Fiction* takes on the 'linear, progressive, Time's-(killing)-arrow mode of the Techno-Heroic', linking linear temporality to established maps and the victors' histories as yang modes in need of change. Inspired by Le Guin's non-Euclidean creative imagination, *Space Crone* carries her writings on gender and feminism by way of ageing, ecology and imagination.

In 1947, Le Guin matriculated at Radcliffe, the women's liberal arts college in Cambridge, Massachusetts. Graduating with a specialism in Renaissance French and Italian literature, she went on to earn a master's at Columbia in

1952. The following year, she received a Fulbright scholarship and travelled to France on the *Queen Mary*. On board, she met Charles Le Guin, another Fulbright scholar and a historian of French history; they married a few months later. Le Guin did not complete her thesis on the poet Jean Lemaire de Belges (Charles finished his doctorate in 1956), but instead turned her focus to writing fiction and poetry, while working as a secretary and French teacher.

After returning from France, the Le Guins settled in Portland, Oregon. Their first child, Elisabeth, was born in 1957, followed by Caroline in 1959. During this time, Le Guin wrote five novels, all of which were rejected by publishers as inaccessible. Charles, then a history professor at Portland State University, helped to care for the children so Le Guin could write. By the time their final child, Theodore, was born in 1964, Le Guin was publishing stories in science fiction and fantasy magazines. In 1966, aged thirty-seven, she published her first novels, *Rocannon's World* and *Planet of Exile*. These introduced readers to the Hainish universe: the ancient, galaxy-spanning Hainish diplomatic corps provide an ironic – even anthropological – eye on the human beings their ancestors had sown throughout the galaxy.

Le Guin's success was secured with the publication in 1968 of *A Wizard of Earthsea*, the first of the six *Earthsea* books. (Parnassus, the small press that published the book, had also published her mother's second book on Ishi.) Le Guin had developed Earthsea as a setting in two short stories – the title of one of these, 'The Rule of Names' (1964), points to her world's linguistic magic – but began work on the novel in response to a request from Parnassus editor Herman Schein, who asked her to write a book for older children, with complete freedom as to its subject and genre. Le Guin, mother of children aged eleven, nine and five, chose to write a coming-of-age story through the figure of Ged, who makes a destructive mistake and, in taking responsibility for his actions, changes Earthsea itself.

This would prove to be Le Guin's narrative as well. When feminists argued that *A Wizard of Earthsea* and *The Dispossessed* (1974) featured male protagonists and male-dominated worlds and powers, she listened to the charge. She sought not only a corrective, but a transformative redress, putting into practice the Taoist principle of Balance as seen in Earthsea. Not only did she increasingly centre women characters, she edited and advocated for anthologies of women science-fiction writers – and challenged those who excluded them, writing in 1987 to an editor who asked her to introduce an all-male anthology: 'I cannot imagine myself blurbing the first of a new series and hence presumably exemplary of the series, which not only contains no writing by women, but the tone of which is so self-contentedly, exclusively male, like a club, or a locker room.' She acknowledged her attraction to adventure fiction's masculinist history, and she connected Ged, the solitary hero, to a chosen family, made up of the characters Tenar, a priestess who prises herself from the princess narrative in *The Tombs of Atuan* (1970); Tehanu, the survivor that she adopts in *Tehanu* (1990); and Dragonfly and other dragons who enlarge the world of Earthsea in *Tales from Earthsea* and *The Other Wind* (both 2001). If Le Guin reimagined the world in her writing, it was because she was always open to her writing being reimagined by the world.

Le Guin's central concern was this inter-affective confluence of right language and right thinking: not in a rigidly moralistic sense, but at the fulcrum of magic, poetry and justice. Offering an auto-ethnography of the writer in the process of changing her mind, her essays move at tree speed towards refining or discerning an idea, through processes of repetition, renunciation, collaborative vision, and questioning.

Published a year after the first Earthsea book, *The Left Hand of Darkness* (1969) is Le Guin's most famous experiment in gender, known for the sentence, 'The king was pregnant.' In being 'about' gender, *Left Hand* is in fact about something more revolutionary: like the Foretelling practice of the genderfluid Gethenians, the subject of gender seems to 'exhibit the perfect uselessness of knowing the answer to the wrong question'. Here, too, Le Guin revised, renounced and listened. She revisited the novel in her essay 'Is Gender Necessary?' then added a commentary on her original work to produce a 'Redux' version. Tuesday Smillie, in her transfeminist reading of *Left Hand*, describes Le Guin's capacity to rethink her thinking as a 'dynamic practice of radical imagination, and its interweaving with a rigorous process of autocritique . . . daring to dream another world and . . . being willing to take ownership of the deficiencies within that dream'.

In Le Guin's essay 'Redux (1988)', she looked back at her 1976 demurral around using 'they' to describe the genderfluid Gethenians, and noted that there was a feminist rationale for, in fact, adopting it:

> I dislike invented pronouns but now dislike them less than the so-called generic pronoun he/him/his, which does in fact exclude women from discourse, and which was an invention of male grammarians, for until the sixteenth century, the English generic singular pronoun was they/them/their, as it still is in English and American colloquial speech. It should be restored to the written language and let the pedants and pundits squeak and gibber in the streets.

Le Guin enjoyed setting the pedants squeaking and gibbering. Here she is describing herself as a man in 'Introducing Myself', a performance lecture first delivered in 1992:

> I am a man. Now you may think that I've made some kind of
> silly mistake about gender, or maybe that I'm trying to fool
> you . . . So when I was born, there actually were only men.
> People were men. They all had one pronoun, his pronoun; so
> that's who I am . . . That's me, the writer, him. I am a man.

Le Guin's observations are always provisional: narra-
tives, she said, are stratagems for mortality – for testing
constructions of 'reality' (hence *Space Crone* includes some
of her short fiction); narrative and form are central to her
political thinking, particularly her feminist challenge to
hierarchies of values.

As the feminist science-fiction critic Marleen Barr notes
of *Searoad* (1991), from which we include two sections, the
novel's setting, 'Klatsand, a real-world town inhabited by
foam and rain women, merges the fantastic and the real;
it is a space for feminist fabulation'. We include two other
fiction works here: 'Sur', one of Le Guin's most puckish
short stories, walks (and sleds) across that space, rewriting
canonical histories and fictions, while novel-within-a-novel
'Dangerous People' is an extension of the compendious
carrier bag that is *Always Coming Home* (1985), a novel that
features a dictionary, critical reflections, naturalist sketches
and playscripts: 'a space for feminist fabulation', it reminds
us, is impossible without the carrying-alongside of 'the
fantastic and the real'.

In 2014, Le Guin accepted the National Book Foundation's
Medal for Distinguished Contribution to American Letters
with a speech that brought the room to its feet. She refused
to be humble and charming; instead, her speech showed
up the invisibility of older women in radical politics,
and the marginalisation of Le Guin's complex political

formation. These words have passed into the popular imaginary:

> We live in capitalism, its power seems inescapable – but then, so did the divine right of kings. Any human power can be resisted and changed by human beings. Resistance and change often begin in art. Very often in our art, the art of words.

How many other writers of science fiction and fantasy have introduced the collected works of a major anarchist thinker? *Space Crone* includes Le Guin's foreword to the writings of Murray Bookchin, whose concept of 'social ecology' has most recently been employed by the Kurdish resistance in Rojava and southern Turkey. She spent ten years researching anarchism to write *The Dispossessed*, one of the fullest fictional realisations of an anarchist society. *The Word for World Is Forest* (1973), her most explicitly polemical novel, a visionary entwining of pacifist, feminist and environmental politics, came out of her experience of protesting the war on Vietnam and its human and more-than-human costs.

Named after her essay of the same title in this volume, *Space Crone* brings together for the first time writings by Le Guin that illustrate the many meanings and dimensions of feminism and gender in her thought. Crossing geographical and temporal expanses, Le Guin the space crone entwines fantasy and science fiction, myth and making. As befits the inventor of the ansible device for simultaneous communication across light-years, Le Guin's method was not linear, but concerned with revisiting and with simultaneity: while texts proceed chronologically by date of publication according to Le Guin's unruly and self-determined copyright dates, the imprint page lists dates of first and collected publication. Le Guin's open-ended method offers an alternative historiography, one that is always in a process of self-editing and iteration.

The graphic novelist Blue Delliquanti has written that they 'always like reading Le Guin's work because she writes stories about things like starships and aliens while asking herself how people from different places or cultures think about them from other perspectives'. Le Guin's writing makes space for other writers, like a canopy tree that feeds and shelters many species. The twenty-first century, as Le Guin put it, has become too yang, moving too far in the direction of the anthropocentro-cene. The emergence from the coronavirus pandemic into the messiness of a symbiotic reality, entangled with ongoing climate catastrophe, economic recession and political confusion, demands moving towards yin: to the interspecies consciousness threaded through her writing.

Two images recur in Le Guin's work: waves (her homage to Virginia Woolf) and trees, which – as in her story 'The Direction of the Road' (1974) – give access to a more-than-human timescale, at once cumulative and slow. Unbound by the codex form, we might arrange *Space Crone* in rings, alluding to the concentric patterning of Le Guin's thinking, moving inwards and outwards from the anti-war, environmental, and anarchist politics that pre-dated (and post-dated) her feminist realisation. Our hope is not to crown Le Guin ruler of the forest, but to enable intergenerational exchanges of nutrients, new growths from old.

Le Guin ends 'Introducing Myself' by observing: 'I am not sure that anybody has invented old women yet; but it might be worth trying.' Le Guin's essays always recognise the etymology of the word *essayer*, 'to try', as well as the belief that there might be something worthwhile in the attempt. That is how we have approached the selection of these essays and stories, recognising that other editors could listen in to Le Guin's lifetime of experience and expression and shape a completely different book. A provisional anthology made as an offering, *Space Crone* holds out to you that most magical of objects: an anarchic, inventive, feminist carrier bag of ideas.

SO MAYER AND SARAH SHIN
January 2023

THE SPACE CRONE
(1976)

The menopause is probably the least glamorous topic imaginable; and this is interesting, because it is one of the very few topics to which cling some shreds and remnants of taboo. A serious mention of menopause is usually met with uneasy silence; a sneering reference to it is usually met with relieved sniggers. Both the silence and the sniggering are pretty sure indications of taboo.

Most people would consider the old phrase 'change of life' a euphemism for the medical term 'menopause', but I, who am now going through the change, begin to wonder if it isn't the other way round. 'Change of life' is too blunt a phrase, too factual. 'Menopause', with its chime-suggestion of a mere pause after which things go on as before, is re-assuringly trivial.

But the change is not trivial, and I wonder how many women are brave enough to carry it out wholeheartedly. They give up their reproductive capacity with more or less of a struggle, and when it's gone they think that's all there is to it. Well, at least I don't get the Curse any more, they say, and the only reason I felt so depressed sometimes was hormones. Now I'm myself again. But this is to evade the real challenge, and to lose, not only the capacity to ovulate, but the opportunity to become a Crone.

In the old days women who survived long enough to attain the menopause more often accepted the challenge. They had, after all, had practice. They had already changed their life radically once before, when they ceased to be virgins and became mature women/wives/matrons/mothers/mistresses/whores/etc. This change involved not only the physiological alterations of puberty – the shift from barren childhood to fruitful maturity – but a socially recognised alteration of being: a change of condition from the sacred to the profane.

With the secularisation of virginity now complete, so that the once awesome term 'virgin' is now a sneer or at best a slightly dated word for a person who hasn't copulated yet, the opportunity of gaining or regaining the dangerous/sacred condition of being at the Second Change has ceased to be apparent.

Virginity is now a mere preamble or waiting room to be got out of as soon as possible; it is without significance. Old age is similarly a waiting room, where you go after life's over and wait for cancer or a stroke. The years before and after the menstrual years are vestigial: the only meaningful condition left to women is that of fruitfulness. Curiously, this restriction of significance coincided with the development of chemicals and instruments that make fertility itself a meaningless or at least secondary characteristic of female maturity. The significance of maturity now is not the capacity to conceive but the mere ability to have sex. As this ability is shared by pubescents and by postclimacterics, the blurring of distinctions and elimination of opportunities is almost complete. There are no rites of passage because there is no significant change. The Triple Goddess has only one face: Marilyn Monroe's, maybe. The entire life of a woman from ten or twelve through seventy or eighty has become secular, uniform, changeless. As there is no longer any virtue in virginity, so there is no longer any meaning in menopause. It requires fanatical determination now to become a Crone.

Women have thus, by imitating the life condition of men, surrendered a very strong position of their own. Men are afraid of virgins, but they have a cure for their own fear and the virgin's virginity: fucking. Men are afraid of Crones, so afraid of them that their cure for virginity fails them; they know it won't work. Faced with the fulfilled Crone, all but the bravest men wilt and retreat, crestfallen and cockadroop.

Menopause Manor is not merely a defensive stronghold, however. It is a house or household, fully furnished with the necessities of life. In abandoning it, women have narrowed their domain and impoverished their souls. There are things the Old Woman can do, say, and think that the Woman cannot do, say, or think. The Woman has to give up more than her menstrual periods before she can do, say, or think them. She has got to change her life.

The nature of that change is now clearer than it used to be. Old age is not virginity but a third and new condition; the virgin must be celibate, but the crone need not. There was a confusion there, which the separation of female sexuality from reproductive capacity, via modern contraceptives, has cleared up. Loss of fertility does not mean loss of desire and fulfilment. But it does entail a change, a change involving matters even more important – if I may venture a heresy – than sex.

The woman who is willing to make that change must become pregnant with herself, at last. She must bear herself, her third self, her old age, with travail and alone. Not many will help her with that birth. Certainly no male obstetrician will time her contractions, inject her with

3

sedatives, stand ready with forceps, and neatly stitch up the torn membranes. It's hard even to find an old-fashioned midwife, these days. That pregnancy is long, that labour is hard. Only one is harder, and that's the final one, the one that men also must suffer and perform.

It may well be easier to die if you have already given birth to others or yourself, at least once before. This would be an argument for going through all the discomfort and embarrassment of becoming a Crone. Anyhow it seems a pity to have a built-in rite of passage and to dodge it, evade it, and pretend nothing has changed. That is to dodge and evade one's womanhood, to pretend one's like a man. Men, once initiated, never get the second chance. They never change again. That's their loss, not ours. Why borrow poverty?

Certainly the effort to remain unchanged, young, when the body gives so impressive a signal of change as the menopause, is gallant; but it is a stupid, self-sacrificial gallantry, better befitting a boy of twenty than a woman of forty-five or fifty. Let the athletes die young and laurel-crowned. Let the soldiers earn the Purple Hearts. Let women die old, white-crowned, with human hearts.

If a space ship came by from the friendly natives of the fourth planet of Altair, and the polite captain of the space ship said, 'We have room for one passenger; will you spare us a single human being, so that we may converse at leisure during the long trip back to Altair and learn from an exemplary person the nature of the race?' – I suppose what most people would want to do is provide them with a fine, bright, brave young man, highly educated and in peak physical condition. A Russian cosmonaut would be ideal (American astronauts are mostly too old). There would surely be hundreds, thousands of volunteers, just such young men, all worthy. But I would not pick any of them. Nor would I pick any of the young women who would volunteer, some out of magnanimity and intellectual courage, others out of a profound conviction that Altair couldn't possibly be any worse for a woman than Earth is.

What I would do is go down to the local Woolworth's, or the local village marketplace, and pick an old woman, over sixty, from behind the costume jewellery counter or the betel-nut booth. Her hair would not be red or blonde or lustrous dark, her skin would not be dewy fresh, she would not have the secret of eternal youth. She might, however, show you a small snapshot of her grandson, who is working in Nairobi. She is a bit vague about where Nairobi is, but extremely proud of the grandson. She has worked hard at small, unimportant jobs all her life, jobs like cooking, cleaning, bringing up kids, selling little objects of adornment or pleasure to other people. She was a virgin once, a long time ago, and then a sexually potent fertile female, and then went through menopause. She has given birth several times and faced death several times – the same times. She is facing the final birth/death a little more nearly and clearly every day now. Sometimes her feet hurt something terrible. She never was educated to anything like her capacity, and that is a shameful waste and a crime against humanity, but so common a crime should not and cannot be hidden from Altair. And anyhow she's not dumb. She has a stock of sense, wit, patience and experiential shrewdness, which the Altaireans might, or might not, perceive as wisdom. If they are wiser than we, then of course we don't know how they'd perceive it. But if they are wiser than we, they may know how to perceive that inmost mind and heart which we, working on mere guess and hope, proclaim to be humane. In any case, since they are curious and kindly, let's give them the best we have to give.

The trouble is, she will be very reluctant to volunteer. 'What would an old woman like me do on Altair?' she'll say. 'You ought to send one of those scientist men, they can talk to those funny-looking green people. Maybe Dr Kissinger should go. What about sending the Shaman?' It will be very hard to explain to her that we want her to go because only a person who has experienced, accepted, and acted the entire human condition – the essential quality of which is Change – can fairly represent humanity. 'Me?' she'll say, just a trifle slyly. 'But I never did anything.'

But it won't wash. She knows, though she won't admit it, that Dr Kissinger has not gone and will never go where she has gone, that the scientists and the shamans have not done what she has done. Into the space ship, Granny.

SUR
(1982)
A Summary Report of the Yelcho Expedition
to the Antarctic, 1909-1910

Although I have no intention of publishing this
report, I think it would be nice if a grandchild of
mine, or somebody's grandchild, happened to find
it some day; so I shall keep it in the leather trunk in the
attic, along with Rosita's christening dress and Juanito's
silver rattle and my wedding shoes and finneskos.

The first requisite for mounting an expedition – money
– is normally the hardest to come by. I grieve that even
in a report destined for a trunk in the attic of a house in
a very quiet suburb of Lima I dare not write the name
of the generous benefactor, the great soul without whose
unstinting liberality the Yelcho Expedition would never
have been more than the idlest excursion into daydream.
That our equipment was the best and most modern – that
our provisions were plentiful and fine – that a ship of the
Chilean government, with her brave officers and gallant
crew, was twice sent halfway round the world for our convenience: all this is due to that benefactor whose name,
alas! I must not say, but whose happiest debtor I shall be
till death.

When I was little more than a child my imagination was
caught by a newspaper account of the voyage of the *Bel-*

gica, which, sailing south from Tierra del Fuego, became beset by ice in the Bellingshausen Sea and drifted a whole year with the floe, the men aboard her suffering a great deal from want of food and from the terror of the unending winter darkness. I read and reread that account, and later followed with excitement the reports of the rescue of Dr Nordenskjold from the South Shetland Isles by the dashing Captain Irizar of the *Uruguay*, and the adventures of the *Scotia* in the Weddell Sea. But all these exploits were to me but forerunners of the British National Antarctic Expedition of 1902-1904, in the *Discovery*, and the wonderful account of that expedition by Captain Scott. This book, which I ordered from London and reread a thousand times, filled me with longing to see with my own eyes that strange continent, last Thule of the South, which lies on our maps and globes like a white cloud, a void, fringed here and there with scraps of coastline, dubious capes, supposititious islands, headlands that may or may not be there: Antarctica. And the desire was as pure as the polar snows: to go, to see – no more, no less. I deeply respect the scientific accomplishments of Captain Scott's expedition, and have read with passionate interest the findings of physicists, meteorologists, biologists, etc.; but having had no training in any science, nor any opportunity for such training, my ignorance obliged me to forgo any thought of adding to the body of scientific knowledge concerning Antarctica; and the same is true for all the members of my expedition. It seems a pity; but there was nothing we could do about it. Our goal was limited to observation and exploration. We hoped to go a little farther, perhaps, and see a little more; if not, simply to go and to see. A simple ambition, I think, and essentially a modest one.

Yet it would have remained less than an ambition, no more than a longing, but for the support and encouragement of my dear cousin and friend Juana —— ——. (I use no surnames, lest this report fall into strangers' hands at last, and embarrassment or unpleasant notoriety thus be brought upon unsuspecting husbands, sons, etc.) I had lent Juana my copy of *The Voyage of the Discovery*, and it was she who, as we strolled beneath our parasols across the Plaza de Arenas after Mass one Sunday in 1908, said, 'Well, if Captain Scott can do it, why can't we?'

It was Juana who proposed that we write Carlota —— in Valparaiso. Through Carlota we met our benefactor, and so obtained our money, our ship, and even the plausible pretext of going on retreat in a Bolivian convent, which some of us were forced to employ (while the rest of us said we were going to Paris for the winter season). And it was my Juana who in the darkest moments remained resolute, unshaken in her determination to achieve our goal.

And there were dark moments, especially in the early months of 1909 – times when I did not see how the Expedition would ever become more than a quarter ton of pemmican gone to waste and a lifelong regret. It was so very hard to gather our expeditionary force together! So few of those we asked even knew what we were talking about – so many thought we were mad, or wicked, or both! And of those few who shared our folly, still fewer were able, when it came to the point, to leave their daily duties and commit themselves to a voyage of at least six months, attended with not inconsiderable uncertainty and danger. An ailing parent; an anxious husband beset by business cares; a child at home with only ignorant or incompetent servants to look after it: these are not responsibilities lightly to be set aside. And those who wished to evade such claims were not the companions we wanted in hard work, risk and privation.

But since success crowned our efforts, why dwell on

the setbacks and delays, or the wretched contrivances and downright lies that we all had to employ? I look back with regret only to those friends who wished to come with us but could not, by any contrivance, get free – those we had to leave behind to a life without danger, without uncertainty, without hope.

On the seventeenth of August, 1909, in Punta Arenas, Chile, all the members of the Expedition met for the first time: Juana and I, the two Peruvians; from Argentina, Zoe, Berta and Teresa; and our Chileans, Carlota and her friends Eva, Pepita and Dolores. At the last moment I had received word that Maria's husband, in Quito, was ill, and she must stay to nurse him, so we were nine, not ten. Indeed, we had resigned ourselves to being but eight, when, just as night fell, the indomitable Zoe arrived in a tiny pirogue manned by Indians, her yacht having sprung a leak just as it entered the Strait of Magellan.

That night before we sailed we began to get to know one another; and we agreed, as we enjoyed our abominable supper in the abominable seaport inn of Punta Arenas, that if a situation arose of such urgent danger that one voice must be obeyed without present question, the unenviable honour of speaking with that voice should fall first upon myself; if I were incapacitated, upon Carlota; if she, then upon Berta. We three were then toasted as 'Supreme Inca', 'La Araucana' and 'The Third Mate', among a lot of laughter and cheering. As it came out, to my very great pleasure and relief, my qualities as a 'leader' were never tested; the nine of us worked things out amongst us from beginning to end without any orders being given by anybody, and only two or three times with recourse to a vote by voice or show of hands. To be sure, we argued a good deal. But then, we had time to argue. And one way or another the arguments always ended up in a decision, upon which action could be taken. Usually at least one person grumbled about the decision, sometimes bitterly. But what is life without grumbling, and the occasional opportunity to say, 'I told you so'? How could one bear housework, or looking after babies, let alone the rigours of sledge-hauling in Antarctica, without grumbling? Officers – as we came to understand aboard the *Yelcho* – are forbidden to grumble; but we nine were, and are, by birth and upbringing, unequivocally and irrevocably, all crew.

Though our shortest course to the southern continent, and that originally urged upon us by the captain of our good ship, was to the South Shetlands and the Bellingshausen Sea, or else by the South Orkneys into the Weddell Sea, we planned to sail west to the Ross Sea, which Captain Scott had explored and described, and from which the brave Ernest Shackleton had returned only the previous autumn. More was known about this region than any other portion of the coast of Antarctica, and though that more was not much, yet it served as some insurance of the safety of the ship, which we felt we had no right to imperil. Captain Pardo had fully agreed with us after studying the charts and our planned itinerary; and so it was westward that we took our course out of the Strait next morning.

Our journey half round the globe was attended by fortune. The little *Yelcho* steamed cheerily along through gale and gleam, climbing up and down those seas of the Southern Ocean that run unbroken round the world. Juana, who had fought bulls and the far more dangerous cows on her family's *estancia*, called the ship 'la vaca valiente', because she always returned to the charge. Once we got over being seasick we all enjoyed the sea voyage, though oppressed at times by the kindly but officious protectiveness of the captain and his officers, who felt that we were only 'safe' when huddled up in the three tiny cabins which they had chivalrously vacated for our use.

We saw our first iceberg much further south than we had looked for it, and saluted it with Veuve Clicquot at dinner. The next day we entered the ice pack, the belt of floes and bergs, broken loose from the land ice and winter-frozen seas of Antarctica, which drifts northward in the spring. Fortune still smiled on us: our little steamer, incapable, with her unreinforced metal hull, of forcing a way into the ice, picked her way from lane to lane without hesitation, and on the third day we were through the pack, in which ships have sometimes struggled for weeks and been obliged to turn back at last. Ahead of us now lay the dark grey waters of the Ross Sea, and beyond that, on the horizon, the remote glimmer, the cloud-reflected whiteness of the Great Ice Barrier.

Entering the Ross Sea a little east of Longitude West 1600, we came in sight of the Barrier at the place where Captain Scott's party, finding a bight in the vast wall of ice, had gone ashore and sent up their hydrogen-gas balloon for reconnaissance and photography. The towering face of the Barrier, its sheer cliffs and azure and violet water-worn caves, all were as described, but the location had changed: instead of a narrow bight there was a considerable bay, full of the beautiful and terrific orca whales playing and spouting in the sunshine of that brilliant southern spring.

Evidently masses of ice many acres in extent had broken away from the Barrier (which – at least for most of its vast extent – does not rest on land but floats on water) since the *Discovery*'s passage in 1902. This put our plan to set up camp on the Barrier itself in a new light; and while we were discussing alternatives, we asked Captain Pardo to take the ship west along the Barrier face towards Ross Island and McMurdo Sound. As the sea was clear of ice and quite calm, he was happy to do so, and, when we sighted the smoke plume of Mount Erebus, to share in our celebration – another half case of Veuve Clicquot.

The *Yelcho* anchored in Arrival Bay, and we went ashore in the ship's boat. I cannot describe my emotions when I set foot on the earth, on that earth, the barren, cold gravel at the foot of the long volcanic slope. I felt elation, impatience, gratitude, awe, familiarity. I felt that I was home at last. Eight Adélie penguins immediately came to greet us with many exclamations of interest not unmixed with disapproval. 'Where on earth have you been? What took you so long? The Hut is around this way. Please come this way. Mind the rocks!' They insisted on our going to visit Hut Point, where the large structure built by Captain Scott's party stood, looking just as in the photographs and drawings that illustrate his book. The area about it, however, was disgusting – a kind of graveyard of seal skins, seal bones, penguin bones and rubbish, presided over by the mad, screaming skua gulls. Our escorts waddled past the slaughterhouse in all tranquillity, and one showed me personally to the door, though it would not go in.

The interior of the hut was less offensive, but very dreary. Boxes of supplies had been stacked up into a kind of room within the room; it did not look as I had imagined it when the *Discovery* party put on their melodramas and minstrel shows in the long winter night. (Much later, we learned that Sir Ernest had rearranged it a good deal when he was there just a year before us.) It was dirty, and had about it a mean disorder. A pound tin of tea was standing open. Empty meat tins lay about; biscuits were spilled on the floor; a lot of dog turds were underfoot – frozen, of course, but not a great deal improved by that. No doubt the last occupants had had to leave in a hurry, perhaps even in a blizzard. All the same, they could have closed the tea tin. But housekeeping, the art of the infinite, is no game for amateurs.

Teresa proposed that we use the hut as our camp. Zoe counterproposed that we set fire to it. We finally shut the door and left it as we had found it. The penguins appeared to approve, and cheered us all the way to the boat.

McMurdo Sound was free of ice, and Captain Pardo now proposed to take us off Ross Island and across to Victoria Land, where we might camp at the foot of the Western Mountains, on dry and solid earth. But those mountains, with their storm-darkened peaks and hanging cirques and glaciers, looked as awful as Captain Scott had found them on his western journey, and none of us felt much inclined to seek shelter among them.

Aboard the ship that night we decided to go back and set up our base as we had originally planned, on the Barrier itself. For all available reports indicated that the clear way south was across the level Barrier surface until one could ascend one of the confluent glaciers to the high plateau, which appears to form the whole interior of the continent. Captain Pardo argued strongly against this plan, asking what would become of us if the Barrier 'calved' – if our particular acre of ice broke away and started to drift northward. 'Well,' said Zoe, 'then you won't have to come so far to meet us.' But he was so persuasive on this theme that he persuaded himself into leaving one of the *Yelcho*'s boats with us when we camped, as a means of escape. We found it useful for fishing, later on.

My first steps on Antarctic soil, my only visit to Ross Island, had not been pleasure unalloyed. I thought of the words of the English poet:

Though every prospect pleases,
And only Man is vile.

14

But then, the backside of heroism is often rather sad; women and servants know that. They know also that the heroism may be no less real for that. But achievement is smaller than men think. What is large is the sky, the earth, the sea, the soul. I looked back as the ship sailed east again that evening. We were well into September now, with ten hours or more of daylight. The spring sunset lingered on the twelve-thousand-foot peak of Erebus and shone rosy gold on her long plume of steam. The steam from our own small funnel faded blue on the twilit water as we crept along under the towering pale wall of ice.

On our return to 'Orca Bay' – Sir Ernest, we learned years later, had named it the Bay of Whales – we found a sheltered nook where the Barrier edge was low enough to provide fairly easy access from the ship. The *Yelcho* put out her ice anchor, and the next long, hard days were spent in unloading our supplies and setting up our camp on the ice, a half kilometre in from the edge: a task in which the *Yelcho*'s crew lent us invaluable aid and interminable advice. We took all the aid gratefully, and most of the advice with salt.

The weather so far had been extraordinarily mild for spring in this latitude; the temperature had not yet gone below -20° Fahrenheit, and there was only one blizzard while we were setting up camp. But Captain Scott had spoken feelingly of the bitter south winds on the Barrier, and we had planned accordingly. Exposed as our camp was to every wind, we built no rigid structures above ground. We set up tents to shelter in while we dug out a series of cubicles in the ice itself, lined them with hay insulation and pine boarding, and roofed them with canvas over bamboo poles, covered with snow for weight and insulation. The big central room was instantly named Buenos Aires by our Argentineans, to whom the centre, wherever one is, is always Buenos Aires. The heating and cooking stove was in Buenos Aires. The storage tunnels and the privy (called Punta Arenas) got some back heat from the stove. The sleeping cubicles opened off Buenos Aires, and were very small, mere tubes into which one crawled feet first; they were lined deeply with hay and soon warmed by one's body warmth. The sailors called them 'coffins' and 'wormholes', and looked with horror on our burrows in the ice. But our little warren or prairie-dog village served us well, permitting us as much warmth and privacy as one could reasonably expect under the circumstances. If the *Yelcho* was unable to get through the ice in February, and we had to spend the winter in Antarctica, we certainly could do so, though on very limited rations. For this coming summer, our base – Sudamérica del Sur, South South America, but we generally called it the Base – was intended merely as a place to sleep, to store our provisions, and to give shelter from blizzards.

To Berta and Eva, however, it was more than that. They were its chief architect-designers, its most ingenious builder-excavators, and its most diligent and contented occupants, forever inventing an improvement in ventilation, or learning how to make skylights, or revealing to us a new addition to our suite of rooms, dug in the living ice. It was thanks to them that our stores were stowed so handily, that our stove drew and heated so efficiently, and that Buenos Aires, where nine people cooked, ate, worked, conversed, argued, grumbled, painted, played the guitar and banjo, and kept the Expedition's library of books and maps, was a marvel of comfort and convenience. We lived there in real amity; and if you simply had to be alone for a while, you crawled into your sleeping hole head first.

Berta went a little further. When she had done all she could to make South South America liveable, she dug out

16

one more cell just under the ice surface, leaving a nearly transparent sheet of ice like a greenhouse roof; and there, alone, she worked at sculptures. They were beautiful forms, some like a blending of the reclining human figure with the subtle curves and volumes of the Weddell seal, others like the fantastic shapes of ice cornices and ice caves. Perhaps they are there still, under the snow, in the bubble in the Great Barrier. There where she made them they might last as long as stone. But she could not bring them north. That is the penalty for carving in water.

Captain Pardo was reluctant to leave us, but his orders did not permit him to hang about the Ross Sea indefinitely, and so at last, with many earnest injunctions to us to stay put – make no journeys – take no risks – beware of frostbite – don't use edge tools – look out for cracks in the ice – and a heartfelt promise to return to Orca Bay on the twentieth of February, or as near that date as wind and ice would permit, the good man bade us farewell, and his crew shouted us a great good-bye cheer as they weighed anchor. That evening, in the long orange twilight of October, we saw the topmast of the *Yelcho* go down the north horizon, over the edge of the world, leaving us to ice, and silence and the Pole.

The ensuing month passed in short practice trips and depot-laying. The life we had led at home, though in its own way strenuous, had not fitted any of us for the kind of strain met with in sledge-hauling at ten or twenty degrees below freezing. We all needed as much working-out as possible before we dared undertake a long haul.

My longest exploratory trip, made with Dolores and Carlota, was southwest towards Mount Markham, and it was a nightmare – blizzards and pressure ice all the way out, crevasses and no view of the mountains when we got there, and white weather and sastrugi all the way back.

17

The trip was useful, however, in that we could begin to estimate our capacities; and also in that we had started out with a very heavy load of provisions, which we depoted at a hundred and a hundred and thirty miles south-south-west of Base. Thereafter other parties pushed on further, till we had a line of snow cairns and depots right down to Latitude 83° 43', where Juana and Zoe, on an exploring trip, had found a kind of stone gateway opening on a great glacier leading south. We established these depots to avoid, if possible, the hunger that had bedevilled Captain Scott's Southern Party, and the consequent misery and weakness. And we also established to our own satisfaction – intense satisfaction – that we were sledgehaulers at least as good as Captain Scott's husky dogs. Of course we could not have expected to pull as much or as fast as his men. That we did so was because we were favoured by much better weather than Captain Scott's party ever met on the Barrier; and also the quantity and quality of our food made a very consider-able difference. I am sure that the fifteen per cent of dried fruits in our pemmican helped prevent scurvy; and the potatoes, frozen and dried according to an ancient Andean Indian method, were very nourishing yet very light and compact – perfect sledging rations. In any case, it was with considerable confidence in our capacities that we made ready at last for the Southern Journey.

The Southern Party consisted of two sledge teams: Juana, Dolores and myself; Carlota, Pepita and Zoe. The support team of Berta, Eva and Teresa set out before us with a heavy load of supplies, going right up onto the glacier to prospect routes and leave depots of supplies for our return journey. We followed five days behind them, and met them returning between Depot Ercilla and Depot Miranda. That 'night' – of course there was no real dark-ness – we were all nine together in the heart of the level plain of ice. It was the fifteenth of November, Dolores's birthday. We celebrated by putting eight ounces of pisco in the hot chocolate, and became very merry. We sang. It is strange now to remember how thin our voices sounded in that great silence. It was overcast, white weather, without shadows and without visible horizon or any feature to break the level; there was nothing to see at all. We had come to a white place on the map, that void, and there we flew and sang like sparrows.

After sleep and a good breakfast the Base Party continued north, and the Southern Party sledged on. The sky cleared presently. High up, thin clouds passed over very rapidly from southwest to northeast, but down on the Barrier it was calm and just cold enough, five or ten degrees below freezing, to give a firm surface for hauling.

On the level ice we never pulled less than eleven miles (seventeen kilometres) a day, and generally fifteen or sixteen miles (twenty-five kilometres). (Our instruments, being British made, were calibrated in feet, miles, degrees Fahrenheit, etc., but we often converted miles to kilometres because the larger numbers sounded more encouraging.) At the time we left South America, we knew only that Mr Shackleton had mounted another expedition to the Antarctic in 1908, had tried to attain the Pole but failed, and had returned to England in June of the current year, 1909. No coherent report of his explorations had yet reached South America when we left; we did not know what route he had gone, or how far he had got. But we were not altogether taken by surprise when, far across the featureless white plain, tiny beneath the mountain peaks and the strange silent flight of the rainbow-fringed cloud wisps, we saw a fluttering dot of black. We turned west from our course to visit it: a snow heap nearly buried by the winter's storms – a flag on a bamboo pole, a mere shred of threadbare cloth – an empty oilcan – and a few footprints standing some inches above the ice. In some conditions of weather the snow compressed under one's weight remains when the surrounding soft snow melts or is scoured away by the wind; and so these reversed footprints had been left standing all these months, like rows of cobbler's lasts – a queer sight.

We met no other such traces on our way. In general I believe our course was somewhat east of Mr. Shackleton's. Juana, our surveyor, had trained herself well and was faithful and methodical in her sightings and readings, but our equipment was minimal – a theodolite on tripod legs, a sextant with artificial horizon, two compasses, and chronometers. We had only the wheel metre on the sledge to give distance actually travelled.

In any case, it was the day after passing Mr Shackleton's waymark that I first saw clearly the great glacier among the mountains to the southwest, which was to give us a pathway from the sea level of the Barrier up to the altiplano, ten thousand feet above. The approach was magnificent: a gateway formed by immense vertical domes and pillars of rock. Zoe and Juana had called the vast ice river that flowed through that gateway the Florence Nightingale Glacier, wishing to honour the British, who had been the inspiration and guide of our Expedition; that very brave and very peculiar lady seemed to represent so much that is best, and strangest, in the island race. On maps, of course, this glacier bears the name Mr Shackleton gave it, the Beardmore.

The ascent of the Nightingale was not easy. The way was open at first, and well marked by our support party, but after some days we came among terrible crevasses, a maze of hidden cracks, from a foot to thirty feet wide and from thirty to a thousand feet deep. Step by step we went, and step by step, and the way always upward now. We were fifteen days on the glacier. At first the weather was hot, up to 20°F, and the hot nights without darkness were wretchedly uncomfortable in our small tents. And all of us suffered more or less from snowblindness just at the time when we wanted clear eyesight to pick our way among the ridges and crevasses of the tortured ice, and to see the wonders about and before us. For at every day's advance more great, nameless peaks came into view in the west and southwest, summit beyond summit, range beyond range, stark rock and snow in the unending noon.

We gave names to these peaks, not very seriously, since we did not expect our discoveries to come to the attention of geographers. Zoe had a gift for naming, and it is thanks to her that certain sketch maps in various suburban South American attics bear such curious features as 'Bolívar's Big Nose', 'I Am General Rosas', 'The Cloudmaker', 'Whose Toe?' and 'Throne of Our Lady of the Southern Cross'. And when at last we got up onto the altiplano, the great interior plateau, it was Zoe who called it the pampa, and maintained that we walked there among vast herds of invisible cattle, transparent cattle pastured on the spindrift snow, their gauchos the restless, merciless winds. We were by then all a little crazy with exhaustion and the great altitude — twelve thousand feet — and the cold and the wind blowing and the luminous circles and crosses surrounding the suns, for often there were three or four suns in the sky, up there.

That is not a place where people have any business to be. We should have turned back; but since we had worked so hard to get there, it seemed that we should go on, at least for a while.

A blizzard came with very low temperatures, so we had to stay in the tents, in our sleeping bags, for thirty hours, a rest we all needed; though it was warmth we needed most, and there was no warmth on that terrible plain anywhere at all but in our veins. We huddled close together all that time. The ice we lay on is two miles thick.

It cleared suddenly and became, for the plateau, good weather: twelve below zero and the wind not very strong. We three crawled out of our tent and met the others crawling out of theirs. Carlota told us then that her group wished to turn back. Pepita had been feeling very ill; even after the rest during the blizzard, her temperature would not rise above 94°. Carlota was having trouble breathing. Zoe was perfectly fit, but much preferred staying with her friends and lending them a hand in difficulties to pushing on towards the Pole. So we put the four ounces of pisco which we had been keeping for Christmas into the breakfast cocoa, and dug out our tents, and loaded our sledges and parted there in the white daylight on the bitter plain.

Our sledge was fairly light by now. We pulled on to the south. Juana calculated our position daily. On the twenty-second of December, 1909, we reached the South Pole. The weather was, as always, very cruel. Nothing of any kind marked the dreary whiteness. We discussed leaving some kind of mark or monument, a snow cairn, a tent pole and flag; but there seemed no particular reason to do so. Anything we could do, anything we were, was insignificant, in that awful place. We put up the tent for shelter for an hour and made a cup of tea, and then struck '90° Camp'. Dolores, standing patient as ever in her sledging harness, looked at the snow; it was so hard frozen that it showed no trace of our footprints coming, and she said, 'Which way?'

'North,' said Juana.

It was a joke, because at that particular place there is no other direction. But we did not laugh. Our lips were cracked with frostbite and hurt too much to let us laugh. So we started back, and the wind at our backs pushed us along, and dulled the knife edges of the waves of frozen snow.

All that week the blizzard wind pursued us like a pack of mad dogs. I cannot describe it. I wished we had not gone to the Pole. I think I wish it even now. But I was glad even then that we had left no sign there, for some man longing to be first might come some day, and find it, and know then what a fool he had been, and break his heart.

We talked, when we could talk, of catching up to Carlota's party, since they might be going slower than we. In fact they had used their tent as a sail to catch the following wind and had got far ahead of us. But in many places they had built snow cairns or left some sign for us; once Zoe had written on the lee side of a ten-foot sastrugi, just as children write on the sand of the beach at Miraflores, 'This Way Out!' The wind blowing over the frozen ridge had left the words perfectly distinct.

In the very hour that we began to descend the glacier, the weather turned warmer, and the mad dogs were left to howl forever tethered to the Pole. The distance that had taken us fifteen days going up we covered in only eight days going down. But the good weather that had aided us descending the Nightingale became a curse down on the Barrier ice, where we had looked forward to a kind of royal progress from depot to depot, eating our fill and taking our time for the last three hundred-odd miles. In a tight place on the glacier I lost my goggles – I was swinging from my harness at the time in a crevasse – and then Juana had broken hers when we had to do some rock climbing coming down to the Gateway. After two days in bright sunlight with only one pair of snow goggles to pass amongst us, we were all suffering badly from snow-blindness. It became acutely painful to keep lookout for landmarks or depot flags, to take sightings, even to study the compass, which had to be laid down on the snow to steady the needle. At Concolorcorvo Depot, where there was a particularly good supply of food and fuel, we gave up, crawled into our sleeping bags with bandaged eyes, and slowly boiled alive like lobsters in the tent exposed to the relentless sun. The voices of Berta and Zoe were the sweetest sound I ever heard. A little concerned about us, they had skied south to meet us. They led us home to Base.

We recovered quite swiftly, but the altiplano left its mark. When she was very little, Rosita asked if a dog 'had bitted Mama's toes'. I told her Yes, a great, white, mad dog named Blizzard! My Rosita and my Juanito heard many stories when they were little, about that fearful dog and how it howled, and the transparent cattle of the invisible gauchos, and a river of ice eight thousand feet high called Nightingale, and how Cousin Juana drank a cup of tea standing on the bottom of the world under seven suns, and other fairy tales.

We were in for one severe shock when we reached Base at last. Teresa was pregnant. I must admit that my first response to the poor girl's big belly and sheepish look was anger – rage – fury. That one of us should have concealed anything, and such a thing, from the others! But Teresa had done nothing of the sort. Only those who had concealed from her what she most needed to know were to blame. Brought up by servants, with four years' schooling in a convent, and married at sixteen, the poor girl was still so ignorant at twenty years of age that she had thought it was 'the cold weather' that made her miss her periods. Even this was not entirely stupid, for all of us on the Southern Journey had seen our periods change or stop altogether as we experienced increasing cold, hunger and fatigue. Teresa's appetite had begun to draw general attention; and then she had begun, as she said pathetically, 'to get fat'. The others were worried at the thought of all the sledge-hauling she had done, but she flourished, and the only problem was her positively insatiable appetite. As well as could be determined from her shy references to her last night on the hacienda with her husband, the baby was due at just about the same time as the *Yelcho*, the twentieth of February. But we had not been back from the Southern Journey two weeks when, on February 14, she went into labour.

Several of us had borne children and had helped with deliveries, and anyhow most of what needs to be done is fairly self-evident; but a first labour can be long and trying, and we were all anxious, while Teresa was frightened out of her wits. She kept calling for her José till she was as hoarse as a skua. Zoe lost all patience at last and said, 'By God, Teresa, if you say 'José!' once more I hope you have a penguin!' But what she had, after twenty long hours, was a pretty little red-faced girl.

Many were the suggestions for that child's name from her eight proud midwife-aunts: Polita, Penguina, McMurdo, Victoria . . . But Teresa announced, after she had had a good sleep and a large serving of pemmican, 'I shall name her Rosa – Rosa del Sur,' Rose of the South. That night we drank the last two bottles of Veuve Clicquot (having finished the pisco at 88° 30' South) in toasts to our little Rose.

On the nineteenth of February, a day early, my Juana came down into Buenos Aires in a hurry. 'The ship,' she said, 'the ship has come,' and she burst into tears – she who had never wept in all our weeks of pain and weariness on the long haul.

Of the return voyage there is nothing to tell. We came back safe.

In 1912 all the world learned that the brave Norwegian Amundsen had reached the South Pole; and then, much later, came the accounts of how Captain Scott and his men had come there after him, but did not come home again.

Just this year, Juana and I wrote to the captain of the *Yelcho*, for the newspapers have been full of the story of his gallant dash to rescue Sir Ernest Shackleton's men from Elephant Island, and we wished to congratulate him, and once more to thank him. Never one word has he breathed of our secret. He is a man of honour, Luis Pardo.

***

I add this last note in 1929. Over the years we have lost touch with one another. It is very difficult for women to meet, when they live so far apart as we do. Since Juana died, I have seen none of my old sledge-mates, though sometimes we write. Our little Rosa del Sur died of the scarlet fever when she was five years old. Teresa had many other children. Carlota took the veil in Santiago ten years ago. We are old women now, with old husbands, and grown children, and grandchildren who might someday like to read about the Expedition. Even if they are rather ashamed of having such a crazy grandmother, they may enjoy sharing in the secret. But they must not let Mr Amundsen know! He would be terribly embarrassed and disappointed. There is no need for him or anyone else outside the family to know. We left no footprints, even.

BRYN MAWR
COMMENCEMENT ADDRESS
(1986)

Thinking about what I should say to you made me think about what we learn in college; and what we unlearn in college; and then how we learn to unlearn what we learned in college and relearn what we unlearned in college, and so on. And I thought how I have learned, more or less well, three languages, all of them English; and how one of these languages is the one I went to college to learn. I thought I was going to study French and Italian, and I did, but what I learned was the language of power – of social power; I shall call it the father tongue.

This is the public discourse, and one dialect of it is speech-making – by politicians, commencement speakers, or the old man who used to get up early in a village in Central California a couple of hundred years ago and say things very loudly on the order of 'People need to be getting up now, there are things we might be doing, the repairs on the sweathouse aren't finished and the tarweed is in seed over on Bald Hill; this is a good time of day for doing things, and there'll be plenty of time for lying around when it gets hot this afternoon.' So everybody would get up grumbling slightly, and some of them would go pick tarweed – probably the women. This is the effect, ideally, of the public discourse. It makes something happen, makes somebody – usually somebody else – do something, or at least it gratifies the ego of the speaker. The difference between our politics and that of a native Californian people is clear in the style of the public discourse. The difference wasn't clear to the white invaders, who insisted on calling any Indian who made a speech a 'chief', because they couldn't comprehend, they wouldn't admit, an authority without supremacy – a non-dominating authority. But it is such an authority that I possess for the brief – we all hope it is decently brief – time I speak to you. I have no right to speak to you. What I have is the responsibility you have given me to speak to you.

The political tongue speaks aloud – and look how radio and television have brought the language of politics right back where it belongs – but the dialect of the father tongue that you and I learned best in college is a written one. It doesn't speak itself. It only lectures. It began to develop when printing made written language common rather than rare, five hundred years ago or so, and with electronic processing and copying it continues to develop and proliferate so powerfully, so dominatingly, that many believe this dialect – the expository and particularly the scientific discourse – is the *highest* form of language, the true language, of which all other uses of words are primitive vestiges.

And it is indeed an excellent dialect. Newton's *Principia* was written in it in Latin, and Descartes wrote Latin and French in it, establishing some of its basic vocabulary, and Kant wrote German in it, and Marx, Darwin, Freud, Boas, Foucault – all the great scientists and social thinkers wrote it. It is the language of thought that seeks objectivity.

I do not say it is the language of rational thought. Reason is a faculty far larger than mere objective thought. When

either the political or the scientific discourse announces itself as the voice of reason, it is playing God, and should be
spanked and stood in the corner. The essential gesture of
the father tongue is not reasoning but distancing – making
a gap, a space, between the subject or self and the object or
other. Enormous energy is generated by that rending, that
forcing of a gap between Man and World. So the continuous growth of technology and science fuels itself; the
Industrial Revolution began with splitting the world-atom,
and still by breaking the continuum into unequal parts
we keep the imbalance from which our society draws the
power that enables it to dominate every other culture, so
that everywhere now everybody speaks the same language
in laboratories and government buildings and headquarters
and offices of business, and those who don't know it or
won't speak it are silent, or silenced, or unheard.

You came here to college to learn the language of power
– to be empowered. If you want to succeed in business,
government, law, engineering, science, education, the
media, if you want to succeed, you have to be fluent in the
language in which 'success' is a meaningful word.

White man speak with forked tongue; white man speak
dichotomy. His language expresses the values of the split
world, valuing the positive and devaluing the negative in
each redivision: subject/object, self/other, mind/body,
dominant/submissive, active/passive, Man/Nature, man/
woman, and so on. The father tongue is spoken from
above. It goes one way. No answer is expected, or heard.

In our Constitution and the works of law, philosophy,
social thought and science, in its everyday uses in the service of justice and clarity, what I call the father tongue
is immensely noble and indispensably useful. When it
claims a privileged relationship to reality, it becomes
dangerous and potentially destructive. It describes with

29

exquisite accuracy the continuing destruction of the planet's ecosystem by its speakers. This word from its vocabulary, 'ecosystem', is a word unnecessary except in a discourse that excludes its speakers from the ecosystem in a subject/object dichotomy of terminal irresponsibility.

The language of the fathers, of Man Ascending, Man the Conqueror, Civilised Man, is not your native tongue. It isn't anybody's native tongue. You didn't even hear the father tongue your first few years, except on the radio or TV, and then you didn't listen, and neither did your little brother, because it was some old politician with hairs in his nose yammering. And you and your brother had better things to do. You had another kind of power to learn. You were learning your mother tongue.

Using the father tongue, I can speak of the mother tongue only, inevitably, to distance it – to exclude it. It is the other, inferior. It is primitive: inaccurate, unclear, coarse, limited, trivial, banal. It's repetitive, the same over and over, like the work called women's work; earthbound, housebound. It's vulgar, the vulgar tongue, common, common speech, colloquial, low, ordinary, plebeian, like the work ordinary people do, the lives common people live. The mother tongue, spoken or written, expects an answer. It is conversation, a word the root of which means 'turning together'. The mother tongue is language not as mere communication but as relation, relationship. It connects. It goes two ways, many ways, an exchange, a network. Its power is not in dividing but in binding, not in distancing but in uniting. It is written, but not by scribes and secretaries for posterity; it flies from the mouth on the breath that is our life and is gone, like the outbreath, utterly gone and yet returning, repeated, the breath the same again always, everywhere, and we all know it by heart. John have you got your umbrella I think it's going to rain. Can you come play with me? If I told you once I told you a hundred times. Things here just aren't the same without Mother, I will now sign your affectionate brother James. Oh what am I going to do? So I said to her I said if he thinks she's going to stand for that but then there's his arthritis poor thing and no work. I love you. I hate you. I hate liver. Joan dear did you feed the sheep, don't just stand around mooning. Tell me what they said, tell me what you did. Oh how my feet do hurt. My heart is breaking. Touch me here, touch me again. Once bit twice shy. You look like what the cat dragged in. What a beautiful night. Good morning, hello, goodbye, have a nice day, thanks. God damn you to hell you lying cheat. Pass the soy sauce please. Oh shit. Is it grandma's own sweet pretty dear? What am I going to tell her? There there don't cry. Go to sleep now, go to sleep . . . Don't go to sleep!

It is a language always on the verge of silence and often on the verge of song. It is the language stories are told in. It is the language spoken by all children and most women, and so I call it the mother tongue, for we learn it from our mothers and speak it to our kids. I'm trying to use it here in public where it isn't appropriate, not suited to the occasion, but I want to speak it to you because we are women and I can't say what I want to say about women in the language of capital-M Man. If I try to be objective I will say, 'This is higher and that is lower,' I'll make a commencement speech about being successful in the battle of life, I'll lie to you; and I don't want to.

Early this spring I met a musician, the composer Pauline Oliveros, a beautiful woman like a grey rock in a streambed; and to a group of us, women, who were beginning to quarrel over theories in abstract, objective language – and I with my splendid Eastern-women's-college training in the father tongue was in the thick of the fight and going for the kill – to us, Pauline, who is sparing with words, said after clearing her throat, 'Offer your experience as your truth.' There was a short silence. When we started talking again, we didn't talk objectively, and we didn't fight. We went back to feeling our way into ideas, using the whole intellect not half of it, talking with one another, which involves listening. We tried to offer our experience to one another. Not claiming something: offering something.

How, after all, can one experience deny, negate, disprove, another experience? Even if I've had a lot more of it, your experience is your truth. How can one being prove another being wrong? Even if you're a lot younger and smarter than me, my being is my truth. I can offer it; you don't have to take it. People can't contradict each other, only words can: words separated from experience for use as weapons, words that make the wound, the split between subject and object, exposing and exploiting the object but disguising and defending the subject.

People crave objectivity because to be subjective is to be embodied, to be a body, vulnerable, violable. Men especially aren't used to that; they're trained not to offer but to attack. It's often easier for women to trust one another, to try to speak our experience in our own language, the language we talk to each other in, the mother tongue; so we empower one another.

But you and I have learned to use the mother tongue only at home or safe among friends, and many men learn not to speak it at all. They're taught that there's no safe place for them. From adolescence on, they talk a kind of degraded version of the father tongue with each other – sports scores, job technicalities, sex technicalities and TV politics. At home, to women and children talking mother tongue, they respond with a grunt and turn on the ball game. They have let themselves be silenced, and dimly they know it, and so resent speakers of the mother tongue; women babble, gabble all the time . . . Can't listen to that stuff.

Our schools and colleges, institutions of the patriarchy, generally teach us to listen to people in power, men or women speaking the father tongue; and so they teach us not to listen to the mother tongue, to what the powerless say, poor men, women, children: not to hear that as valid discourse.

I am trying to unlearn these lessons, along with other lessons I was taught by my society, particularly lessons concerning the minds, work, works and being of women. I am a slow unlearner. But I love my unteachers – the feminist thinkers and writers and talkers and poets and artists and singers and critics and friends, from Wollstonecraft and Woolf through the furies and glories of the seventies and eighties – I celebrate here and now the women who for two centuries have worked for our freedom, the unteachers, the unmasters, the unconquerors, the unwarriors, women who have at risk and at high cost offered their experience as truth. 'Let us NOT praise famous women!' Virginia Woolf scribbled in a margin when she was writing *Three Guineas*, and she's right, but still I have to praise these women and thank them for setting me free in my old age to learn my own language.

The third language, my native tongue, which I will never know though I've spent my life learning it: I'll say some words now in this language. First a name, just a person's name, you've heard it before. Sojourner Truth. That name is a language in itself. But Sojourner Truth spoke the unlearned language; about a hundred years ago, talking it in a public place, she said, 'I have been forty years a slave and forty years free and would be here forty years more to have equal rights for all.' Along at the end of her talk she said, 'I wanted to tell you a mite about Woman's Rights, and so I came out and said so. I am sittin' among you to watch; and every once and awhile I will come out and tell you what time of night it is.' She said, 'Now I will do a little singing. I have not heard any singing since I came here.'*

Singing is one of the names of the language we never learn, and here for Sojourner Truth is a little singing. It was written by Joy Harjo of the Creek people and is called 'The Blanket Around Her'.†

maybe it is her birth
which she holds close to herself
or her death
which is just as inseparable
and the white wind
that encircles her is a part
just as
the blue sky
hanging in turquoise from her neck

oh woman
remember who you are
woman
it is the whole earth

So what am I talking about with this 'unlearned language' – poetry, literature? Yes, but it can be speeches and sci-

---

* Sojourner Truth, in *The Norton Anthology of Literature by Women*, ed. Sandra M. Gilbert and Susan Gubar (New York: W.W. Norton & Co., 1985).
† Joy Harjo, 'The Blanket Around Her,' in *That's What She Said: Contemporary Poetry and Fiction by Native American Women*, ed. Rayna Green (Bloomington: Indiana University Press, 1984).

ence, any use of language when it is spoken, written, read, heard as art, the way dancing is the body moving as art. In Sojourner Truth's words you hear the coming together, the marriage of the public discourse and the private exper- ience, making a power, a beautiful thing, the true discourse of reason. This is a wedding and welding back together of the alienated consciousness that I've been calling the father tongue and the undifferentiated engagement that I've been calling the mother tongue. This is their baby, this baby talk, the language you can spend your life trying to learn.

We learn this tongue first, like the mother tongue, just by hearing it or reading it; and even in our overcrowded, underfunded public high schools they still teach *A Tale of Two Cities* and *Uncle Tom's Cabin*; and in college you can take four solid years of literature, and even creative writing courses. But. It is all taught as if it were a dialect of the father tongue.

Literature takes shape and life in the body, in the womb of the mother tongue: always: and the Fathers of Cult- ure get anxious about paternity. They start talking about legitimacy. They steal the baby. They ensure by every means that the artist, the writer, is male. This involves intellect- ual abortion by centuries of women artists, infanticide of works by women writers, and a whole medical corps of sterilising critics working to purify the Canon, to reduce the subject matter and style of literature to something Ernest Hemingway could have understood.

But this is our native tongue, this is our language they're stealing: we can read it and we can write it, and what we bring to it is what it needs, the woman's tongue, that earth and savour, that relatedness, which speaks dark in the mother tongue but clear as sunlight in women's poetry, and in our novels and stories, our letters, our journals, our speeches. If Sojourner Truth, forty years a slave, knew she

35

had the right to speak that speech, how about you? Will you let yourself be silenced? Will you listen to what men tell you, or will you listen to what women are saying? I say the Canon has been spiked, and while the Eliots speak only to the Lowells and the Lowells speak only to God, Denise Levertov comes stepping westward quietly, speaking to us.[*]

> There is no savor
> more sweet, more salt
>
> than to be glad to be
> what, woman,
>
> and who, myself,
> I am, a shadow
>
> that grows longer as the sun
> moves, drawn out
>
> on a thread of wonder.
> If I bear burdens
>
> they begin to be remembered
> as gifts, goods, a basket
>
> of bread that hurts
> my shoulders but closes me
>
> in fragrance. I can
> eat as I go.

As I've been using the word 'truth' in the sense of 'trying

[*] Denise Levertov, 'Stepping Westward', in Norton Anthology.

hard not to lie', so I use the words 'literature', 'art', in the sense of 'living well, living with skill, grace, energy' – like carrying a basket of bread and smelling it and eating as you go. I don't mean only certain special products made by specially gifted people living in specially privileged garrets, studios and ivory towers – 'High' Art; I mean also all the low arts, the ones men don't want. For instance, the art of making order where people live. In our culture this activity is not considered an art, it is not even considered work. 'Do you work?' – and she, having stopped mopping the kitchen and picked up the baby to come answer the door, says, 'No, I don't work.' People who make order where people live are by doing so stigmatised as unfit for 'higher' pursuits; so women mostly do it, and among women, poor, uneducated or old women more often than rich, educated and young ones. Even so, many people want very much to keep house but can't, because they're poor and haven't got a house to keep, or the time and money it takes, or even the experience of ever having seen a decent house, a clean room, except on TV. Most men are prevented from housework by intense cultural bias; many women actually hire another woman to do it for them because they're scared of getting trapped in it, ending up like the woman they hire, or like that woman we all know who's been pushed so far over by cultural bias that she can't stand up, and crawls around the house scrubbing and waxing and spraying germ killer on the kids. But even on her kneebones, where you and I will never join her, even she has been practising as best she knows how a great, ancient, complex and necessary art. That our society devalues it is evidence of the barbarity, the aesthetic and ethical bankruptcy, of our society.

As housekeeping is an art, so is cooking and all it involves – it involves, after all, agriculture, hunting, herding

37

. . . So is the making of clothing and all it involves . . . And so on; you see how I want to revalue the word 'art' so that when I come back as I do now to talking about words it is in the context of the great arts of living, of the woman carrying the basket of bread, bearing gifts, goods. Art not as some ejaculative act of ego but as a way, a skilful and powerful way of being in the world. I come back to words because words are my way of being in the world, but meaning by language as art a matter infinitely larger than the so-called High forms. Here is a poem that tries to translate six words by Hélène Cixous, who wrote *The Laugh of the Medusa*; she said, 'Je suis là où ça parle', and I squeezed those six words like a lovely lemon and got out all the juice I could, plus a drop of Oregon vodka.

I'm there where
it's talking
Where that speaks I
am in that talking place
Where
that says
my being is
Where
my being there
is speaking
I am
And so
laughing
in a stone ear

The stone ear that won't listen, won't hear us, and blames us for its being stone . . . Women can babble and chatter like monkeys in the wilderness, but the farms and orchards and gardens of language, the wheatfields of art –

men have claimed these, fenced them off: No Trespassing, it's a man's world, they say. And I say,

oh woman
remember who you are
woman
it is the whole earth

We are told, in words and not in words, we are told by their deafness, by their stone ears, that our experience, the life experience of women, is not valuable to men – therefore not valuable to society, to humanity. We are valued by men only as an element of their experience, as things experienced; anything we may say, anything we may do, is recognised only if said or done in their service.

One thing we incontestably do is have babies. So we have babies as the male priests, lawmakers and doctors tell us to have them, when and where to have them, how often, and how to have them; so that is all under control. But we are not to talk about having babies, because that is not part of the experience of men and so nothing to do with reality, with civilisation, and no concern of art. – A rending scream in another room. And Prince Andrey comes in and sees his poor little wife dead bearing his son – Or Levin goes out into his fields and thanks his God for the birth of his son – And we know how Prince Andrey feels and how Levin feels and even how God feels, but we don't know what happened. Something happened, something was done, which we know nothing about. But what was it? Even in novels by women we are only just beginning to find out what it is that happens in the other room – what women do.

Freud famously said, 'What we shall never know is what a woman wants.' Having paused thoughtfully over the syntax of that sentence, in which WE are plural but 'a woman' apparently has no plural, no individuality – as we might read that a cow must be milked twice a day or a gerbil is a nice pet – WE might go on then to consider whether WE know anything about, whether WE have ever noticed, whether WE have ever asked a woman what she *does* – what women do.

Many anthropologists, some historians, and others have indeed been asking one another this question for some years now, with pale and affrighted faces – and they are beginning also to answer it. More power to them. The social sciences show us that speakers of the father tongue are capable of understanding and discussing the doings of the mothers, if they will admit the validity of the mother tongue and listen to what women say.

But in society as a whole the patriarchal mythology of what 'a woman' does persists almost unexamined, and shapes the lives of women. 'What are you going to do when you get out of school?' 'Oh, well, just like any other woman, I guess I want a home and family' – and that's fine, but what is this home and family just like other women's? Dad at work, mom home, two kids eating apple pie? This family, which our media and now our government declare to be normal and impose as normative, this nuclear family now accounts for seven per cent of the arrangements women live in in America. Ninety-three per cent of women don't live that way. They don't do that. Many wouldn't if you gave it to them with bells on. Those who want that, who believe it's their one true destiny – what's their chance of achieving it? They're on the road to Heartbreak House.

But the only alternative offered by the patriarchal mythology is that of the Failed Woman – the old maid, the barren woman, the castrating bitch, the frigid wife, the lezzie, the libber, the Unfeminine, so beloved of misogynists both male and female.

Now indeed there are women who want to be female men; their role model is Margaret Thatcher, and they're ready to dress for success, carry designer briefcases, kill for promotion, and drink the Right Scotch. They want to buy into the man's world, whatever the cost. And if that's true desire, not just compulsion born of fear, OK; if you can't lick 'em join 'em. My problem with that is that I can't see it as a good life even for men, who invented it and make all the rules. There's power in it, but not the kind of power I respect, not the kind of power that sets anybody free. I hate to see an intelligent woman voluntarily double herself up to get under the bottom line. Talk about crawling! And when she talks, what can she talk but father tongue? If she's the mouthpiece for the man's world, what has she got to say for herself?

Some women manage it – they may collude, but they don't sell out as women; and we know that when they speak for those who, in the man's world, are the others: women, children, the poor . . .

But it is dangerous to put on Daddy's clothes, though not, perhaps, as dangerous as it is to sit on Daddy's knees.

There's no way you can offer your experience as your truth if you deny your experience, if you try to be a mythical creature, the dummy woman who sits there on Big Daddy's lap. Whose voice will come out of her prettily hinged jaw? Who is it says yes all the time? Oh yes, yes, I will. Oh I don't know, you decide. Oh I can't do that. Yes hit me, yes rape me, yes save me, oh yes. That is how A Woman talks, the one in What-we-shall-never-know-is-what-A-Woman-wants.

A Woman's place, need I say, is in the home, plus at her volunteer work or the job where she's glad to get sixty cents for doing what men get paid a dollar for but that's because she's always on pregnancy leave or childcare? No! A Woman is home caring for her children! Even if she can't. Trapped in this well-built trap, A Woman blames her mother for luring her into it, while ensuring that her own daughter never gets out; she recoils from the idea of sisterhood and doesn't believe women have friends, because it probably means something unnatural, and anyhow, A Woman is afraid of women. She's a male construct, and she's afraid women will deconstruct her. She's afraid of everything, because she can't change. Thighs forever thin and shining hair and shining teeth and she's my Mom, too, all seven per cent of her. And she never grows old.

There are old women – little old ladies, as people always say; little bits, fragments of the great dummy statue goddess A Woman. Nobody hears if old women say yes or no, nobody pays them sixty cents for anything. Old men run things. Old men run the show, press the buttons, make the wars, make the money. In the man's world, the old man's world, the young men run and run and run until they drop, and some of the young women run with them. But old women live in the cracks, between the walls, like roaches, like mice, a rustling sound, a squeaking. Better lock up the cheese, boys. It's terrible, you turn up a corner of civilisation and there are all these old women running around on the wrong side . . .

I say to you, you know, you're going to get old. And you can't hear me. I squeak between the walls. I've walked through the mirror and am on the other side, where things are all backwards. You may look with a good will and a generous heart, but you can't see anything in the mirror but your own face; and I, looking from the dark side and seeing your beautiful young faces, see that that's how it should be.

But when you look at yourself in the mirror, I hope you see yourself. Not one of the myths. Not a failed man – a person who can never succeed because success is basically defined as being male – and not a failed goddess, a person desperately trying to hide herself in the dummy Woman, the image of men's desires and fears. I hope you look away from those myths and into your own eyes, and see your own strength. You're going to need it. I hope you don't try to take your strength from men, or from a man. Second-hand experience breaks down a block from the car lot. I hope you'll take and make your own soul; that you'll feel your life for yourself pain by pain and joy by joy; that you'll feed your life, eat, 'eat as you go' – you who nourish, be nourished!

If being a cog in the machine or a puppet manipulated by others isn't what you want, you can find out what you want, your needs, desires, truths, powers, by accepting your own experience as a woman, as this woman, this body, this person, your hungry self. On the maps drawn by men there is an immense white area, terra incognita, where most women live. That country is all yours to explore, to inhabit, to describe.

But none of us lives there alone. Being human isn't something people can bring off alone; we need other people in order to be people. We need one another.

If a woman sees other women as Medusa, fears them, turns a stone ear to them, these days, all her hair may begin to stand up on end hissing: Listen, listen, listen! Listen to other women, your sisters, your mothers, your grandmothers – if you don't hear them how will you ever understand what your daughter says to you?

And the men who can talk, converse with you, not trying to talk through the dummy Yes-Woman, the men who can accept your experience as valid – when you find such

43

a man, love him, honour him! But don't obey him. I don't think we have any right to obedience. I think we have a responsibility to freedom.

And especially to freedom of speech. Obedience is silent. It does not answer. It is contained. Here is a disobedient woman speaking, Wendy Rose of the Hopi and Miwok people, saying in a poem called 'The Parts of a Poet'*

> parts of me are pinned
> to earth, parts of me
> undermine song, parts
> of me spread on the water,
> parts of me form a rainbow
> bridge, parts of me follow
> the sandfish, parts of me
> are a woman who judges.

Now this is what I want: I want to hear your judgements. I am sick of the silence of women. I want to hear you speaking all the languages, offering your experience as your truth, as human truth, talking about working, about making, about unmaking, about eating, about cooking, about feeding, about taking in seed and giving out life, about killing, about feeling, about thinking; about what women do; about what men do; about war, about peace; about who presses the buttons and what buttons get pressed and whether pressing buttons is in the long run a fit occupation for human beings. There's a lot of things I want to hear you talk about.

This is what I don't want: I don't want what men have. I'm glad to let them do their work and talk their talk. But I do not want and will not have them saying or thinking

* Wendy Rose, 'The Parts of a Poet', in *That's What She Said*.

or telling us that theirs is the only fit work or speech for human beings. Let them not take our work, our words, from us. If they can, if they will, let them work with us and talk with us. We can all talk mother tongue, we can all talk father tongue, and together we can try to hear and speak that language which may be our truest way of being in the world, we who speak for a world that has no words but ours.

I know that many men and even women are afraid and angry when women do speak, because in this barbaric society, when women speak truly they speak subversively – they can't help it: if you're underneath, if you're kept down, you break out, you subvert. We are volcanoes. When we women offer our experience as our truth, as human truth, all the maps change. There are new mountains.

That's what I want – to hear you erupting. You young Mount St Helenses who don't know the power in you – I want to hear you. I want to listen to you talking to each other and to us all: whether you're writing an article or a poem or a letter or teaching a class or talking with friends or reading a novel or making a speech or proposing a law or giving a judgement or singing the baby to sleep or discussing the fate of nations, I want to hear you. Speak with a woman's tongue. Come out and tell us what time of night it is! Don't let us sink back into silence. If we don't tell our truth, who will? Who'll speak for my children, and yours?

So I end with the end of a poem by Linda Hogan of the Chickasaw people, called 'The Women Speaking'.

Daughters, the women are speaking.
They arrive
over the wise distances
on perfect feet.
Daughters, I love you.

IS GENDER NECESSARY?
(REDUX)
(1976/1988)

Editors' note: 'Is Gender Necessary' first appeared in *Aurora: Beyond Equality*, an anthology of feminist science fiction edited by Vonda McIntyre and Susan Janice Anderson, published by Fawcett Gold Medal in 1976, which also included the first published excerpt of Marge Piercy's *Woman on the Edge of Time* and James Tiptree Jr's award-winning novella *Houston, Houston, Do You Read?* Le Guin included the essay in the first edition of *The Language of the Night*, published by Putnam in 1979. In her introduction to the book's 1989 Women's Press UK edition, she writes that:

> In general, I feel that revising published work is taboo . . . [In this case] the changes I wanted to make were not aesthetic improvements, but had a moral and intellectual urgency to me . . . Within a few years [of its publication], I came to disagree completely with some of the things I said in ['Is Gender Necessary?'], but there they were in print, and all I could do was writhe in deserved misery as the feminists told me off and the masculinists patted my head. Clearly it would have been unethical to rewrite the 1976 text, to disappear it; so it appears here, complete, but with remarks and annotations and self-recriminations from later years. I do hope I don't have to do this again in the nineties.

There were no subsequent revisions to the essay, although her revision to the essay also prompted her, as she notes in the introduction, to change the 'so-called "generic pronoun" *he* [throughout the book] . . . following context, euphony or whim, to *they, she, one, I, you* or *we*'. The 1989 UK edition presents 'Is

Gender Necessary? (Redux)' in two columns: the 1976 essay on the left-hand side of the page, and, in the right-hand column, titled 'Redux (1988)', the annotations in the same font size but italicised, and numbered as notes.

I n the mid-1960s the women's movement was just be-ginning to move again, after a fifty-year halt. There was a groundswell gathering. I felt it, but I didn't know it was a groundswell; I just thought it was something wrong with me. I considered myself a feminist: I didn't see how you could be a thinking woman and not be a feminist; but I had never taken a step beyond the ground gained for us by Emmeline Pankhurst and Virginia Woolf.*

Along about 1967, I began to feel a certain unease, a need to step on a little farther, perhaps, on my own. I began to want to define and understand the meaning of sexuality and the meaning of gender, in my life and in our society. Much had gathered in the unconscious – both personal and collective – which must either be brought up into consciousness or else turn destructive. It was that same need, I think, that had led de Beauvoir to write *The Second Sex*, and Friedan to write *The Feminine Mystique*, and that was, at the same time, leading Kate Millett and others to write their books, and to create the new feminism. But I was not a theoretician, a political thinker or activist, or a sociologist. I was and am a fiction writer. The way I did my thinking was to write a novel. That novel, *The Left Hand of Darkness*, is the record of my consciousness, the process

* Feminism has enlarged its ground and strengthened its theory and practice immensely, and enduringly, in these past twenty years; but has anyone actually taken a step 'beyond' Virginia Woolf? The image, implying an ideal of 'progress', is not one I would use now.

of my thinking.

Perhaps, now that we have all[†] moved on to a plane of heightened consciousness about these matters, it might be of some interest to look back on the book, to see what it did, what it tried to do, and what it might have done, insofar as it is a 'feminist'[‡] book. (Let me repeat the last qualification, once. The fact is that the real subject of the book is not feminism or sex or gender or anything of the sort; as far as I can see, it is a book about betrayal and fidelity. That is why one of its two dominant sets of symbols is an extended metaphor of winter, of ice, snow, cold: the winter journey. The rest of this discussion will concern only half, the lesser half, of the book.)[§]

It takes place on a planet called Gethen, whose human inhabitants differ from us in their sexual physiology. Instead of our continuous sexuality, the Gethenians have an oestrous period, called kemmer. When they are not in kemmer, they are sexually inactive and impotent; they are also androgynous. An observer in the book describes the cycle:

> In the first phase of kemmer [the individual] remains completely androgynous. Gender, and potency, are not attained in isolation . . . Yet the sexual impulse is tremendously strong in this phase, controlling the entire personality . . . When the

[†] Well, quite a lot of us, anyhow.

[‡] Strike the quotation marks from the word 'feminist', please.

[§] This parenthesis is overstated; I was feeling defensive, and resentful that critics of the book insisted upon talking only about its 'gender problems', as if it were an essay not a novel. 'The fact is that the real subject of the book is . . .' This is bluster. I had opened a can of worms and was trying hard to shut it. 'The fact is' however, that there are other aspects to the book, which are involved with its sex/gender aspects quite inextricably.

individual finds a partner in kemmer, hormonal secretion is further stimulated (most importantly by touch – secretion? scent?) until in one partner either a male or female hormonal dominance is established. The genitals engorge or shrink accordingly, foreplay intensifies, and the partner, triggered by the change, takes on the other sexual role (apparently without exception) . . . Normal individuals have no predisposition to either sexual role in kemmer; they do not know whether they will be the male or the female, and have no choice in the matter . . . The culminant phase of kemmer lasts from two to five days, during which sexual drive and capacity are at maximum. It ends fairly abruptly, and if conception has not taken place, the individual returns to the latent phase and the cycle begins anew. If the individual was in the female role and was impregnated, hormonal activity of course continues, and for the gestation and lactation periods this individual remains female . . . With the cessation of lactation the female becomes once more a perfect androgyne. No physiological habit is established, and the mother of several children may be the father of several more.

Why did I invent these peculiar people? Not just so that the book could contain, halfway through it, the sentence 'The king was pregnant' – though I admit that I am fond of that sentence. Not, certainly not, to propose Gethen as a model for humanity. I am not in favour of genetic alteration of the human organism – not at our present level of understanding. I was not recommending the Gethenian sexual setup: I was using it. It was a heuristic device, a thought-experiment. Physicists often do thought-experiments. Einstein shoots a light ray through a moving elevator; Schrödinger puts a cat in a box. There is no elevator, no cat, no box. The experiment is performed, the question is asked, in the mind. Einstein's elevator, Schrödinger's cat, my Gethenians, are simply a way of thinking. They are questions, not answers; process, not stasis. One of the essential functions of science fiction, I think, is precisely this kind of question-asking: reversals of a habitual way of thinking, metaphors for what our language has no words for as yet, experiments in imagination.

The subject of my experiment, then, was something like this: Because of our lifelong social conditioning, it is hard for us to see clearly what, besides purely physiological form and function, truly differentiates men and women. Are there real differences in temperament, capacity, talent, psychic process, etc.? If so, what are they? Only comparative ethnology offers, so far, any solid evidence on the matter, and the evidence is incomplete and often contradictory. The only going social experiments that are truly relevant are the kibbutzim and the Chinese communes, and they too are inconclusive – and hard to get unbiased information about. How to find out? Well, one can always put a cat in a box. One can send an imaginary, but conventional, indeed rather stuffy, young man from Earth into an imaginary culture which is totally free of sex roles because there is no, absolutely no, physiological sex distinction. I eliminated gender, to find out what was left. Whatever was left would be, presumably, simply human. It would define the area that is shared by men and women alike.

I still think that this was a rather neat idea. But as an experiment, it was messy. All results were uncertain; a repetition of the experiment by someone else, or by myself seven years later, would probably* give quite different results. Scientifically, this is most disreputable. That's all right; I am not a scientist. I play the game where the rules keep changing.

* Strike the word 'probably' and replace it with 'certainly'.

51

Among these dubious and uncertain results, achieved as I thought, and wrote, and wrote, and thought, about my imaginary people, three appear rather interesting to me.

First: the absence of war. In the thirteen thousand years of recorded history on Gethen, there has not been a war. The people seem to be as quarrelsome, competitive and aggressive as we are; they have fights, murders, assassinations, feuds, forays and so on. But there have been no great invasions by peoples on the move, like the Mongols in Asia or the whites in the New World: partly because Gethenian populations seem to remain stable in size, they do not move in large masses, or rapidly. Their migrations have been slow, no one generation going very far. They have no nomadic peoples, and no societies that live by expansion and aggression against other societies. Nor have they formed large, hierarchically governed nation-states, the mobilizable entity that is the essential factor in modern war. The basic unit all over the planet is a group of two hundred to eight hundred people, called a hearth, a structure founded less on economic convenience than on sexual necessity (there must be others in kemmer at the same time), and therefore more tribal than urban in nature, though overlaid and interwoven with a later urban pattern. The hearth tends to be communal, independent, and somewhat introverted. Rivalries between hearths, as between individuals, are channelled into a socially approved form of aggression called *shifgrethor*, a conflict without physical violence, involving one-upmanship, the saving and losing of face – conflict ritualised, stylised, controlled. When shifgrethor breaks down there may be physical violence, but it does not become mass violence, remaining limited, personal. The active group remains small. The dispersive trend is as strong as the cohesive. Historically, when hearths gathered into a nation for economic reasons, the cellular pattern still dominated the centralised one. There might be a king and a parliament, but authority was not enforced so much by might as by the use of shifgrethor and intrigue, and was accepted as custom, without appeal to patriarchal ideals of divine right, patriotic duty, etc. Ritual and parade were far more effective agents of order than armies or police. Class structure was flexible and open; the value of the social hierarchy was less economic than aesthetic, and there was no great gap between rich and poor. There was no slavery or servitude. Nobody owned anybody. There were no chattels. Economic organization was rather communistic or syndicalistic than capitalistic, and was seldom highly centralised.

During the timespan of the novel, however, all this is changing. One of the two large nations of the planet is becoming a genuine nation-state, complete with patriotism and bureaucracy. It has achieved state capitalism and the centralisation of power, authoritarian government, and a secret police; and it is on the verge of achieving the world's first war.

Why did I present the first picture, and show it in the process of changing to a different one? I am not sure. I think it is because I was trying to show a balance – and the delicacy of a balance. To me the 'female principle' is, or at least historically has been, basically anarchic. It values order without constraint, rule by custom not by force. It has been the male who enforces order, who constructs power structures, who makes, enforces and breaks laws. On Gethen, these two principles are in balance: the decentralising against the centralising, the flexible against the rigid, the circular against the linear. But balance is a precarious state, and at the moment of the novel the balance, which had leaned toward the 'feminine', is tipping the other way.

Second: the absence of exploitation. The Gethenians do not rape their world. They have developed a high technology, heavy industry, automobiles, radios, explosives, etc., but they have done so very slowly, absorbing their technology rather than letting it overwhelm them. They have no myth of Progress at all. Their calendar calls the current year always the Year One, and they count backward and forward from that.

In this, it seems that what I was after again was a balance: the driving linearity of the 'male', the pushing forward to the limit, the logicality that admits no boundary – and the circularity of the 'female', the valuing of patience, ripeness, practicality, livableness. A model for this balance, of course, exists on Earth: Chinese civilisation over the past six millennia. (I did not know when I wrote the book that the parallel extends even to the calendar; the Chinese historically never had a linear dating system such as the one that starts with the birth of Christ.)

Third: the absence of sexuality as a continuous social factor. For four-fifths of the month, a Gethenian's sexuality plays no part of all in his social life (unless he's pregnant); for the other one-fifth, it dominates him absolutely. In kemmer, one must have a partner, it is imperative. (Have you ever lived in a small apartment with a tabby-cat in heat?) Gethenian society fully accepts this imperative. When a Gethenian has to make love, he does make love, and everybody expects him to, and approves of it.

But still, human beings are human beings, not cats. Despite our continuous sexuality and our intense self-domestication (domesticated animals tend to be promiscuous, wild animals pair-bonding, familial or tribal in their mating), we are very seldom truly promiscuous. We do have rape, to be sure – no other animal has equalled us there. We have mass rape, when an army (male, of course)

54

invades; we have prostitution, promiscuity controlled by economics; and sometimes ritual abreactive promiscuity controlled by religion; but in general we seem to avoid genuine licence. At most we award it as a prize to the Alpha Male, in certain situations; it is scarcely ever permitted to the female without social penalty. It would seem, perhaps, that the mature human being, male or female, is not satisfied by sexual gratification without psychic involvement, and in fact may be *afraid of it*, to judge by the tremendous variety of social, legal and religious controls and sanctions exerted over it in all human societies. Sex is a great mana, and therefore the immature society, or psyche, sets great taboos about it. The mature culture, or psyche, can integrate these taboos or laws into an internal ethical code, which, while allowing great freedom, does not permit the treatment of another person as an object. But, however irrational or rational, there is always a code.

Because the Gethenians cannot have sexual intercourse unless both partners are willing, because they cannot rape or be raped, I figured that they would have less fear and guilt about sex than we tend to have; but still it is a problem for them, in some ways more than for us, because of the extreme, explosive, imperative quality of the oestrous phase. Their society would have to control it, though it might move more easily than we from the taboo stage to the ethical stage. So the basic arrangement, I found, in every Gethenian community, is that of the kemmerhouse, which is open to anyone, in kemmer, native or stranger, so that he can find a partner.* Then there are various customary (not legal) institutions, such as the kemmering group, a group who choose to come together during kemmer as a regular thing; this is like the primate tribe, or group

* Read: . . . so that they can find sexual partners.

marriage. Or there is the possibility of vowing kemmering, which is marriage, pair-bonding for life, a personal commitment without legal sanction. Such commitments have intense moral and psychic significance, but they are not controlled by Church or State. Finally, there are two forbidden acts, which might be taboo or illegal or simply considered contemptible, depending on which of the regions of Gethen you are in: first, you don't pair off with a relative of a different generation (one who might be your own parent or child); second, you may mate, but not vow kemmering, with your own sibling. These are the old incest prohibitions. They are so general among us – and with good cause, I think, not so much genetic as psychological – that they seemed likely to be equally valid on Gethen.

These three 'results', then, of my experiment, I feel were fairly clearly and successfully worked out, though there is nothing definitive about them.

In other areas where I might have pressed for at least such plausible results, I see now a failure to think things through, or to express them clearly. For example, I think I took the easy way in using such familiar governmental structures as a feudal monarchy and a modern-style bureaucracy for the two Gethenian countries that are the scene of the novel. I doubt that Gethenian governments, rising out of the cellular hearth, would resemble any of our own so closely. They might be better, they might be worse, but they would certainly be different.

I regret even more certain timidities or ineptnesses I showed in following up the psychic implications of Gethenian physiology. Just for example, I wish I had known Jung's work when I wrote the book: so that I could have decided whether a Gethenian had no animus or anima, or both, or an animum* . . . But the central failure in this area comes up in the frequent criticism I receive, that the

Gethenians seem like men, instead of menwomen.

This rises in part from the choice of pronoun. I call Gethenians 'he' because I utterly refuse to mangle English by inventing a pronoun for 'he/she'.[†]

'He' is the generic pronoun, damn it, in English. (I envy the Japanese, who, I am told, do have a he/she pronoun.) But I do not consider this really very important.[‡]

The pronouns wouldn't matter at all if I had been clev-

---

[*] For another example (and Jung wouldn't have helped with this, more likely hindered) I quite unnecessarily locked the Gethenians into heterosexuality. It is a naively pragmatic view of sex that insists that sexual partners must be of opposite sex! In any kemmerhouse homosexual practice would, of course, be possible and acceptable and welcomed – but I never thought to explore this option; and the omission, alas, implies that sexuality is heterosexuality. I regret this very much.

[†] This 'utter refusal' of 1968 restated in 1976 collapsed, utterly, within a couple of years more. I still dislike invented pronouns, but now dislike them less than the so-called generic pronoun he/him/his, which does in fact exclude women from discourse; and which was an invention of male grammarians, for until the sixteenth century the English generic singular pronoun was they/them/their, as it still is in English and American colloquial speech. It should be restored to the written language, and let the pedants and pundits squeak and gibber in the streets.

In a screenplay of *The Left Hand of Darkness* written in 1985, I referred to Gethenians not pregnant or in kemmer by the invented pronouns a/un/a's, modeled on a British dialect. These would drive the reader mad in print, I suppose; but I have read parts of the book aloud using them, and the audience was perfectly happy, except that they pointed out that the subject pronoun, 'a' pronounced 'uh' [Ch], sounds too much like 'I' said with a Southern accent.

[‡] I now consider it very important.

erer at showing the 'female' component of the Gethenian characters in action.*

Unfortunately, the plot and structure that arose as I worked the book out cast the Gethenian protagonist, Estraven, almost exclusively into roles that we are culturally conditioned to perceive as 'male' — a prime minister (it takes more than even Golda Meir and Indira Gandhi to break a stereotype), a political schemer, a fugitive, a prison-breaker, a sledge-hauler . . . I think I did this because I was privately delighted at watching, not a man, but a manwoman, do all these things, and do them with considerable skill and flair. But, for the reader, I left out too much. One does not see Estraven as a mother, with his children,† in any role that we automatically perceive as 'female': and therefore, we tend to see him as a man.‡ This is a real flaw in the book, and I can only be very grateful to those readers, men and women, whose willingness to participate in the experiment led them to fill in that omission with the work of their own imagination, and to see Estraven as I saw him,§ as man and woman, familiar and different, alien and utterly human.

It seems to be men, more often than women, who thus complete my work for me: I think because men are often more willing to identify as they read with poor, confused, defensive Genly, the Earthman, and therefore to participate in his painful and gradual discovery of love.◊

Finally, the question arises, Is the book a Utopia? It seems

* If I had realised how the pronouns I used shaped, directed, controlled my own thinking, I might have been 'cleverer'.
† Strike 'his'.
‡ Place 'him' in quotation marks, please.
§ Read: . . . as I did.

to me that it is quite clearly not; it poses no practicable alternative to contemporary society, since it is based on an imaginary, radical change in human anatomy. All it tries to do is open up an alternative viewpoint, to widen the imagination, without making any very definite suggestions as to what might be seen from that new viewpoint. The most it says is, I think, something like this: If we were socially ambisexual, if men and women were completely and genuinely equal in their social roles, equal legally and economically, equal in freedom, in responsibility, and in self-esteem, then society would be a very different thing. What our problems might be, God knows; I only know we would have them. But it seems likely that our central problem would not be the one it is now: the problem of exploitation – exploitation of the woman, of the weak, of the earth. Our curse is alienation, the separation of yang from yin.¶ Instead of a search for balance and integration, there is a struggle for dominance. Divisions are insisted upon, interdependence is denied. The dualism of value that destroys us, the dualism of superior/inferior, ruler/ruled, owner/owned, user/used, might give way to what seems to me, from here, a much healthier, sounder, more promising modality of integration and integrity.

◊ I now see it thus: Men were inclined to be satisfied with the book, which allowed them a safe trip into androgyny and back, from a conventionally male viewpoint. But many women wanted it to go further, to dare more, to explore androgyny from a woman's point of view as well as a man's. In fact, it does so, in that it was written by a woman. But this is admitted directly only in the chapter 'The Question of Sex', the only voice of a woman in the book. I think women were justified in asking more courage of me and a more rigorous thinking-through of implications.

¶ – and the moralization of yang as good, of yin as bad.

THE FISHERWOMAN'S
DAUGHTER
(1988)

I read the first version of this paper at Brown University and at Miami
University in Ohio, and revised it heavily to read at Wesleyan College in
Georgia. Then I wrote it all over again to read at Portland State Univers-
ity. I have a feeling I read it somewhere else, but can't reconstruct where.
When I went to Tulane to be a Mellon Fellow – to be precise, a quarter of
a Mellon – I re-wrote it again, and that version, which I pretended was
definitive, appeared in Tulane's series of Mellon papers, under the title 'A
Woman Writing'. Asked to give the talk in a benefit series in San Francisco,
I decided to include more about my mother, whose writing life was lived in
the Bay Area; and that led to another full revision.

In preparing the manuscript of this book, I came to the immense folder
containing the five – in places identical, in places widely differing – type-
scripts of the talk; and I thought, 'If I have to rewrite that thing once more
I will die.' So I merely included the latest version, without rereading it. My
ruthless editor would have none of that. 'Pusillanimous woman,' she said,
'what about all the bits you left out?' 'What about them?' I snarled. 'I
think if we just put them together it will work,' said she. 'Show me,' said I,
craftily. So she did. I hope it does.*

What pleases me most about the piece, after so much work on it, is that
I can look on it at last as a collaboration. The responses from the various
audiences I read it to, both questions in the lecture hall and letters afterwards, guided and clarified my thinking and saved me from many follies

and omissions. The present re-collation and editing has given me back the whole thing – not shapely and elegant, but a big crazy quilt. And that was my working title for it when I first began gathering material: 'Crazy Quilt'. That name hints again at collaboration, which is what I saw myself as doing as I pieced together the works and words of so many other writers – ancestors, strangers, friends.

'So of course,' wrote Betty Flanders, pressing her heels rather deeper in the sand, 'there was nothing for it but to leave.'
That is the first sentence of Virginia Woolf's *Jacob's Room*.[†] It is a woman writing. Sitting on the sand by the sea, writing. It's only Betty Flanders, and she's only writing a letter. But first sentences are doors to worlds. This world of Jacob's room, so strangely empty at the end of the book when the mother stands in it holding out a pair of her son's old shoes and saying, 'What am I to do with these?' – this is a world in which the first thing one sees is a woman, a mother of children, writing.

On the shore, by the sea, outdoors, is that where women write? Not at a desk, in a writing room? Where does a woman write, what does she look like writing, what is my image, your image, of a woman writing? I asked my friends: 'A woman writing: what do you see?' There would

[*] Editors' note: Le Guin's comments refer to her preparation of the essay for *Dancing At the Edge of the World*; the 'ruthless editor' refers not to the Silver Press team, but to her editor for the collection at Paladin, or, more likely, her inner editor.
[†] Virginia Woolf, *Jacob's Room* (London: The Hogarth Press).
[‡] The edition of *Little Women* I used was my mother's and is now my daughter's. It was published in Boston by Little, Brown, undated, around the turn of the century, and Merrill's fine drawings have also been reproduced in other editions.

be a pause, then the eyes would light up, seeing. Some sent me to paintings, Fragonard, Cassatt, but mostly these turned out to be paintings of a woman reading or with a letter, not actually writing or reading the letter but looking up from it with unfocused eyes: Will he never return? Did I remember to turn off the pot roast? . . . Another friend responded crisply, 'A woman writing is taking dictation.' And another said, 'She's sitting at the kitchen table, and the kids are yelling.'

And that last is the image I shall pursue. But first let me tell you my own first answer to my question: Jo March. From the immediacy, the authority, with which Frank Merrill's familiar illustrations of Little Women‡ came to my mind as soon as I asked myself what a woman writing looks like, I know that Jo March must have had real influence upon me when I was a young scribbler. I am sure she has influenced many girls, for she is not, like most 'real' authors, either dead or inaccessibly famous; nor, like so many artists in books, is she set apart by sensitivity or suffering or general superlativity; nor is she, like most authors in novels, male. She is close as a sister and common as grass. As a model, what does she tell scribbling girls? I think it worthwhile to follow the biography of Jo March the Writer until we come to that person of whom, as a child and until quite recently, I knew almost nothing: Louisa May Alcott.

We first meet Jo as a writer when sister Amy vengefully burns her manuscript, 'the loving work of several years. It seemed a small loss to others, but to Jo it was a dreadful calamity.' How could a book, several years' work, be 'a small loss' to anyone? That horrified me. How could they ask Jo to forgive Amy? At least she nearly drowns her in a frozen lake before forgiving her. At any rate, some chapters later Jo is

> very busy in the garret . . . seated on the old sofa, writing busily, with her papers spread out on a trunk before her . . . Jo's desk up here was an old tin kitchen . . .

– the OED says, 'New England: a roasting pan.' So Jo's room of her own at this stage is a garret furnished with a sofa, a roasting pan and a rat. To any twelve-year-old, heaven.

> Jo scribbled away till the last page was filled, when she signed her name with a flourish . . . Lying back on the sofa she read the manuscript carefully through, making dashes here and there, and putting in many exclamation points, which looked like little balloons; then she tied it up with a smart red ribbon and sat a minute looking at it with a sober, wistful expression, which plainly showed how earnest her work had been.

I am interested here by the counterplay of a deflating irony – the scribbling, the dashes, the balloons, the ribbon – and that wistful earnestness.

Jo sends her story to a paper, it is printed, and she reads it aloud to her sisters, who cry at the right places. Beth asks, 'Who wrote it?'

> The reader suddenly sat up, cast away the paper, displaying a flushed countenance, and with a funny mixture of solemnity and excitement, replied, in a loud voice, 'Your sister.'

The March family makes a great fuss, 'for these foolish, affectionate people made a jubilee of every little household joy' – and there again is deflation, a writer's first publication reduced to a 'little household joy'. Does it not debase art? And yet does it not also, by refusing the heroic tone, refuse to inflate art into something beyond the reach of any 'mere girl'?

So Jo goes on writing; here she is some years later, and I quote at length, for this is the central image.

Every few weeks she would shut herself up in her room, put on her scribbling suit, and 'fall into a vortex', as she expressed it, writing away at her novel with all her heart and soul, for till that was finished she could find no peace. Her 'scribbling suit' consisted of a black woolen pinafore on which she could wipe her pen at will, and a cap of the same material, adorned with a cheerful red bow . . . This cap was a beacon to the inquiring eyes of her family, who during these periods kept their distance, merely popping in their heads semi-occasionally to ask, with interest, 'Does genius burn, Jo?' They did not always venture even to ask this question, but took an observation of the cap, and judged accordingly. If this expressive article of dress was drawn low upon the forehead, it was a sign that hard work was going on; in exciting moments it was pushed rakishly askew; and when despair seized the author it was plucked wholly off and cast upon the floor. At such times the intruder silently withdrew; and not until the red bow was seen gayly erect upon the gifted brow, did anyone dare address Jo.

She did not think herself a genius by any means; but when the writing fit came on, she gave herself up to it with entire abandon, and led a blissful life, unconscious of want, care, or bad weather, while she sat safe and happy in an imaginary world, full of friends almost as real and dear to her as any in the flesh. Sleep forsook her eyes, meals stood untasted, day and night were all too short to enjoy the happiness which blessed her only at such times, and made these hours worth living, even if they bore no other fruit. The divine afflatus usually lasted a week or two, and then she emerged from her vortex, hungry, sleepy, cross, or despondent.

This is a good description of the condition in which the

work of art is done. This is the real thing – domesticated. The cap and bow, the facetious turns and the disclaimers, deflate without degrading, and allow Alcott to make a rather extraordinary statement: that Jo is doing something very important and doing it entirely seriously and that there is nothing unusual about a young woman's doing it. This passion of work and this happiness which blessed her in doing it are fitted without fuss into a girl's commonplace life at home. It may not seem much; but I don't know where else I or many other girls like me, in my generation or my mother's or my daughters', were to find this model, this validation.

Jo writes romantic thrillers and they sell; her father shakes his head and says, 'Aim at the highest and never mind the money,' but Amy remarks, 'The money is the best part of it.' Working in Boston as a governess-seamstress, Jo sees that 'money conferred power: money and power, therefore, she resolved to have; not to be used for herself alone,' our author's author hastily adds, 'but for those whom she loved more than self . . . She took to writing sensation stories.' Her first visit to the editorial office of the *Weekly Volcano* is handled lightly, but the three men treat her as a woman who has come to sell herself – true Lévi-Straussians, to whom what a woman does is entirely subsumed in woman as commodity. Refusing shame, Jo writes on, and makes money by her writing; admitting shame, she does not 'tell them at home'.

> Jo soon found that her innocent experience had given her but few glimpses of the tragic world which underlies society; so, regarding it in a business light, she set about supplying her deficiencies with characteristic energy . . . She searched newspapers for accidents, incidents, and crimes; she excited the suspicions of public librarians by asking for works on poisons;

she studied faces in the street, and characters good, bad, and indifferent all about her . . . Much describing of other people's passions and feelings set her to studying and speculating about her own – a morbid amusement, in which healthy young minds do not voluntarily indulge –

but which one might think appropriate, even needful, to the young novelist? However, 'wrongdoing always brings its own punishment, and when Jo most needed hers, she got it'.

Her punishment is administered by the Angel in the House, in the form of Professor Bhaer. Knowing that she is soiling her pure soul, he attacks the papers she writes for: 'I do not like to think that good young girls should see such things.' Jo weakly defends them, but when he leaves she rereads her stories, three months' work, and burns them. Amy doesn't have to do it for her any more; she can destroy herself. Then she sits and wonders: 'I almost wish I hadn't any conscience, it's so inconvenient!' A cry from the heart of Bronson Alcott's daughter. She tries a pious tale and a children's story, which don't sell, and gives up: she 'corked up her inkstand'.

Beth dies, and trying to replace her, Jo tries 'to live for others' – finally driving her mother to say, 'Why don't you write? That always used to make you happy.' So she does, and she writes both well and successfully – until Professor Bhaer returns and marries her, evidently the only way to make her stop writing. She has his two boys to bring up, and then her two boys, and then all those Little Men in the next volume; at the end of *Little Women*, in the chapter called 'Harvest Time', she says, 'I haven't given up the hope that I may write a good book yet, but I can wait.'

The harvest seems indefinitely deferred. But, in Rachel Blau Du Plessis' phrase,* Jo writes beyond the ending. In

67

the third volume, *Jo's Boys*, she has gone back in middle age
to writing, and is rich and famous. There is realism, tough-
ness, and comedy in the descriptions of her managing the
household, mothering the teenagers, writing her chapters,
and trying to avoid the celebrity hunters. In fact this, like
the whole story of Jo the Writer, is quite close to Louisa
Alcott's own story, with one large difference. Jo marries
and has children. Lu did not.

And yet she undertook the responsibility for a family,
some of whom were as improvident and self-centred as
any baby. There is a heartbreaking note in her journal[†] for
April 1869, when she was suffering a 'bad spell' of mer-
cury poisoning (the calomel given her to cure fever when
she was a nurse in the Civil War made her sick the rest of
her life):

> Very poorly. Feel quite used up. Don't care much for myself,
> as rest is heavenly, even with pain; but the family seems so
> panic-stricken and helpless when I break down, that I try to
> keep the mill going. Two short tales for L., $50; two for Ford,
> $20; and did my editorial work, though two months are un-
> paid for. Roberts wants a new book, but am afraid to get into
> a vortex lest I fall ill.

Alcott used the same word Jo used for her passions of
writing; here are a couple of journal passages comparable
to the 'vortex' passage in *Little Women*.

---

[*] Rachel Blau Du Plessis, *Writing Beyond the Ending: Narrative Strategies of
Twentieth-Century Women Writers* (London: Harvester Press Ltd, 1986).
[†] *Louisa May Alcott: Her Life, Letters and Journals* (Boston:
Roberts Brothers, 1890).

August 1860 – 'Moods' [a novel]. Genius burned so fiercely that for four weeks I wrote all day and planned nearly all night, being quite possessed by my work. I was perfectly happy, and seemed to have no wants.

February 1861 – Another turn at 'Moods', which I remodeled. From the 2d to the 25th I sat writing, with a run at dusk; could not sleep, and for three days was so full of it I could not stop to get up. Mother made me a green silk cap with a red bow, to match the old green and red party wrap, which I wore as a 'glory cloak'. Thus arrayed sat in a grove of manuscripts, 'living for immortality' as May said. Mother wandered in and out with cordial cups of tea, worried because I couldn't eat. Father thought it fine, and brought his reddest apples and hardest cider for my Pegasus to feed upon . . . It was very pleasant and queer while it lasted . . .

And it is pleasant to see how the family whose debts she slaved to pay off, and which she strove so to protect and keep in comfort, tried to protect and help her in return.

Like so many women of her century, then, Lu Alcott had a family, though she did not marry. 'Liberty is a better husband than love to many of us,' she wrote, but in fact she had very little liberty, in the sense of freedom from immediate, personal responsibilities. She even had a baby – her sister May's. Dying from complications of childbirth, May asked the beloved older sister, then forty-eight, to bring up little Lu; which she did until her death eight years later.

All this is complex, more complex, I think, than one tends to imagine; for the Victorian script calls for a clear choice – either books or babies for a woman, not both. And Jo seems to make that choice. I was annoyed at myself when I realised that I had forgotten Jo's survival as a writer – that my memory, except for one nagging scrap that

69

led me to look up *Jo's Boys* at last, had followed the script. That, of course, is the power of the script: you play the part without knowing it.

Here is a classic – a scriptural – description of a writing woman, the mother of children, one of whom is just now in the process of falling down the stairs.

Mrs Jellyby was a pretty, very diminutive, plump woman, of from forty to fifty, with handsome eyes, though they had a curious habit of seeming to look a long way off . . . [She] had very good hair, but was too much occupied with her African duties to brush it . . . We could not help noticing that her dress didn't nearly meet up the back, and that the open space was railed across with a latticework of stay-laces – like a summer-house.

The room, which was strewn with papers and nearly filled by a great writing-table covered with similar litter, was, I must say, not only very untidy, but very dirty. We were obliged to take notice of that with our sense of sight, even while, with our sense of hearing, we followed the poor child who had tumbled downstairs: I think into the back kitchen, where somebody seemed to stifle him. But what principally struck us was a jaded and unhealthy-looking, though by no means plain girl, at the writing-table, who sat biting the feather of her pen, and staring at us. I suppose nobody ever was in such a state of ink.[*]

I will, with difficulty, restrain myself from reading you the rest of *Bleak House*. I love Dickens and will defend his Mrs Jellyby and her correspondence with Borrioboola-Gha as an eternal send-up of those who meddle with foreign morals while remaining oblivious to the misery under

[*] Charles Dickens, *Bleak House*.

their nose. But I observe also that he uses a woman to make this point, probably because it was, and is, safe: few readers would question the assumption that a woman should put family before public responsibility, or that if she does work outside the 'private sphere' she will be neglectful of her house, indifferent to the necks of her children, and incompetent to fasten her clothing. Mrs Jellyby's daughter is saved from her enforced 'state of ink' by marriage, but Mrs Jellyby will get no help from her husband, a man so inert that their marriage is described as the union of mind and matter. Mrs Jellyby is a joy to me, she is drawn with so much humour and good nature; and yet she troubles me, because behind her lurks the double standard. Nowhere among Dickens' many responsible, intelligent women is there one who does real artistic or intellectual work, to balance Mrs Jellyby and reassure us that it isn't what she does but how she does it that is deplorable. And yet the passage just quoted is supposed to have been written by a woman – the character Esther Summerson. Esther herself is a problem. How does she write half Dickens' novel for him while managing Bleak House and getting smallpox and everything else? We never catch her at it. As a woman writing, Esther is invisible. She is not in the script.

There may be a sympathetic portrait of a woman writer with children in a novel written by a man. I have read versions of this paper in Rhode Island, Ohio, Georgia, Louisiana, Oregon, and California, and asked each audience please to tell me if they knew of any such. I wait in hope. Indeed, the only sympathetic picture of a woman novelist in a man's novel that I know is the protagonist of *Diana of the Crossways*. Meredith shows her writing novels for her living, doing it brilliantly, and finding her freedom in her professionalism. But, self-alienated by a disastrous infatuation, she begins to force her talent and can't

71

work – the script apparently being that love is incidental for a man, everything for a woman. At the end, well off and happily married, she is expecting a baby, but not, it appears, a book. All the same, Diana still stands, nearly a century later, quite alone at her crossways.

Invisibility as a writer is a condition that affects not only characters but authors, and even the children of authors. Take Elizabeth Barrett Browning, whom we have consistently put to bed with a spaniel, ignoring the fact that when she wrote *Aurora Leigh* she was the healthy mother of a healthy four-year-old – ignoring, in fact, the fact that she wrote *Aurora Leigh*, a book about being a woman writer, and how difficult one's own true love can make it for one.

Here is a woman who had several children and was a successful novelist, writing a letter to her husband about a hundred and fifty years ago, or maybe last night:

> If I am to write, I must have a room to myself, which shall be my room. All last winter I felt the need of some place where I could go and be quiet. I could not [write in the dining room] for there was all the setting of tables and clearing up of tables and dressing and washing of children, and everything else going on, and . . . I never felt comfortable there, though I tried hard. Then if I came into the parlor where you were, I felt as if I were interrupting you, and you know you sometimes thought so too.[*]

What do you mean? Not at all! Silly notion! Just like a woman!

Fourteen years and several more children later, that woman wrote *Uncle Tom's Cabin* – most of it at the kitchen table.

[*] Harriet Beecher Stowe, 1841, quoted in Tillie Olsen, *Silences* (London: Virago Press, 1980).

A room of one's own – yes. One may ask why Mr Harriet Beecher Stowe got a room to himself to write in, while the woman who wrote the most morally effective American novel of the nineteenth century got the kitchen table. But then one may also ask why she accepted the kitchen table. Any self-respecting man would have sat there for five minutes and then stalked out shouting, 'Nobody can work in this madhouse, call me when dinner's ready!' But Harriet, a self-respecting woman, went on getting dinner with the kids all underfoot and writing her novels. The first question, to be asked with awe, is surely, How? But then, Why? Why are women such patsies?

The quick-feminist-fix answer is that they are victims of and/or accomplices with the patriarchy, which is true but doesn't really get us anywhere new. Let us go to another woman novelist for help. I stole the Stowe quotation (and others) from Tillie Olsen's *Silences*, a book to which this paper stands in the relation of a loving but undutiful daughter – Hey, Ma, that's a neat quotation, can I wear it? This next one I found for myself, in *The Autobiography* of Margaret Oliphant, a fascinating book, from the generation just after Stowe. Oliphant was a successful writer very young, married, had three kids, went on writing, was left a widow with heavy debts and the three kids plus her brother's three kids to bring up, did so, went on writing . . . When her second book came out, she was still, like Jo March, a girl at home.

> I had a great pleasure in writing, but the success and the three editions had no particular effect upon my mind . . . I had nobody to praise me except my mother and [brother] Frank, and their applause – well, it was delightful, it was everything in the world – it was life – but it did not count. They were part of me,

and I of them, and we were all in it.*

I find that extraordinary. I cannot imagine any male auth-
or saying anything like that at all. There is a key here –
something real that has been neglected, been hidden, been
denied.

> . . . The writing ran through everything. But then it was also
> subordinate to everything, to be pushed aside for any little
> necessity. I had no table even to myself, much less a room to
> work in, but sat at the corner of the family table with my writ-
> ing-book, with everything going on as if I had been making
> a shirt instead of writing a book . . . My mother sat always at
> needlework of some kind, and talked to whoever might be
> present, and I took my share in the conversation, going on all
> the same with my story, the little groups of imaginary persons,
> these other talks evolving themselves quite undisturbed.

How's that for an image, the group of imaginary people
talking in the imaginary room in the real room among the
real people talking, and all of it going on perfectly quiet
and unconfused . . . But it's shocking. She can't be a real
writer. Real writers writhe on solitary sofas in cork-lined
rooms, agonising after le mot juste – don't they?

> My study, all the study I have ever attained to, is the little sec-
> ond drawing-room where all the life of the house goes on . . .

– you recall that she was bringing up six children? –

* This and the subsequent connected passages are from the
Autobiography and Letters of Mrs Margaret Oliphant, edited by Mrs Harry
Coghill (Leicester: Leicester University Press, The Victorian Library,
1974).

74

. . . and I don't think I have ever had two hours undisturbed (except at night when everybody is in bed) during my whole literary life. Miss Austen, I believe, wrote in the same way, and very much for the same reason; but at her period the natural flow of life took another form. The family were half ashamed to have it known that she was not just a young lady like the others, doing her embroidery. Mine were quite pleased to magnify me and to be proud of my work, but always with a hidden sense that it was an admirable joke . . .

– perhaps artists cast off their families and go to the South Sea Islands because they want to be perceived as heroes and their families think they are funny? –

. . . a hidden sense that it was an admirable joke, and no idea that any special facilities or retirement was necessary. My mother would have felt her pride much checked, almost humiliated, if she had conceived that I stood in need of any artificial aids of that description. That would at once have made the work unnatural to her eyes, and also to mine.

Oliphant was a proud Scotswoman, proud of her work and her strength; yet she wrote nonfiction potboilers rather than fight her male editors and publishers for better pay for her novels. So, as she says bitterly, 'Trollope's worst book was better paid than my best.' Her best is said to be *Miss Marjoribanks*, but I have never yet been able to get a copy of it; it was disappeared, along with all her other books. Thanks to publishers such as Virago we can now get Oliphant's *Hester*, a stunning novel, and *Kirsteen* and a few others, but they are still taught, so far as I know, only in women's studies courses; they are not part of the Canon of English Literature, though Trollope's potboilers are. No book by a woman who had children has ever been included in that august list.

I think Oliphant gives us a glimpse of why a novelist might not merely endure writing in the kitchen or the parlour amidst the children and the housework, but might endure it willingly. She seems to feel that she profited, that her writing profited, from the difficult, obscure, chancy connection between the art work and the emotional/ manual/managerial complex of skills and tasks called 'housework', and that to sever that connection would put the writing itself at risk, would make it, in her word, unnatural.

The received wisdom of course is just the opposite: that any attempt to combine art work with housework and family responsibility is impossible, unnatural. And the punishment for unnatural acts, among the critics and the Canoneers, is death.

What is the ethical basis of this judgement and sentence upon the housewife-artist? It is a very noble and austere one, with religion at its foundation: it is the idea that the artist must sacrifice himself to his art. (I use the pronoun advisedly.) His responsibility is to his work alone. It is a motivating idea of the Romantics, it guides the careers of poets from Rimbaud to Dylan Thomas to Richard Hugo, it has given us hundreds of hero figures, typical of whom is James Joyce himself and his Stephen Dedalus. Stephen sacrifices all 'lesser' obligations and affections to a 'high-er' cause, embracing the moral irresponsibility of the soldier or the saint. This heroic stance, the Gauguin Pose, has been taken as the norm – as natural to the artist – and artists, both men and women, who do not assume it have tended to feel a little shabby and second-rate.

Not, however, Virginia Woolf. She observed factually that the artist needs a small income and a room to work in, but did not speak of heroism. Indeed, she said, 'I doubt that a writer can be a hero. I doubt that a hero can be a writer.' And when I see a writer assume the full heroic posture, I incline to agree. Here, for example, is Joseph Conrad:

> For twenty months I wrestled with the Lord for my creation . . . mind and will and conscience engaged to the full, hour after hour, day after day . . . a lonely struggle in a great isolation from the world. I suppose I slept and ate the food put before me and talked connectedly on suitable occasions, but I was never aware of the even flow of daily life, made easy and noiseless for me by a silent, watchful, tireless affection.*

A woman who boasted that her conscience had been engaged to the full in such a wrestling match would be called to account by both women and men; and women are now calling men to account. What 'put food' before him? What made daily life so noiseless? What in fact was this 'tireless affection', which sounds to me like an old Ford in a junkyard but is apparently intended as a delicate gesture towards a woman whose conscience was engaged to the full, hour after hour, day after day, for twenty months, in seeing to it that Joseph Conrad could wrestle with the Lord in a very relatively great isolation, well housed, clothed, bathed and fed?

Conrad's 'struggle' and Jo March/Lu Alcott's 'vortex' are descriptions of the same kind of all-out artistic work; and in both cases the artist is looked after by the family. But I feel an important difference in their perceptions. Where Alcott receives a gift, Conrad asserts a right; where she is taken into the vortex, the creative whirlwind, becoming part of it, he wrestles, struggles, seeking mastery. She is

* Joseph Conrad, quoted in Olsen.

a participant; he is a hero. And her family remain individuals, with cups of tea and timid inquiries, while his is depersonalised to 'an affection'.

Looking for a woman writer who might have imitated this heroic infantilism, I thought of Gertrude Stein, under the impression that she had used Alice Toklas as a 'wife' in this utilitarian sense; but that, as I should have guessed, is an anti-lesbian canard. Stein certainly took hero-artist poses and indulged an enormous ego, but she played fair; and the difference between her domestic partnership and that of Joyce or Conrad is illuminating. And indeed, lesbianism has given many artists the network of support they need – for there is a heroic aspect to the practice of art; it is lonely, risky, merciless work, and every artist needs some kind of moral support or sense of solidarity and validation.

The artist with the least access to social or aesthetic solidarity or approbation has been the artist-housewife. A person who undertakes responsibility both to her art and to her dependent children, with no 'tireless affection' or even tired affection to call on, has undertaken a full-time double job that can be simply, practically, destroyingly impossible. But that isn't how the problem is posed – as a recognition of immense practical difficulty. If it were, practical solutions would be proposed, beginning with childcare. Instead the issue is stated, even now, as a moral one, a matter of ought and ought not. The poet Alicia Ostriker puts it neatly: 'That women should have babies rather than books is the considered opinion of Western civilisation. That women should have books rather than babies is a variation on that theme.'*

Freud's contribution to this doctrine was to invest it with such a weight of theory and mythology as to make it appear a primordial, unquestionable fact. It was of course Freud who, after telling his fiancée what it is a woman wants, said that what we shall never know is what a woman wants. Lacan is perfectly consistent in following him, if I as a person without discourse may venture to say so. A culture or a psychology predicated upon man as human and woman as other cannot accept a woman as artist. An artist is an autonomous, choice-making self: to be such a self a woman must unwoman herself. Barren, she must imitate the man – imperfectly, it goes without saying.[†]

Hence the approbation accorded Austen, the Brontës, Dickinson and Plath, who though she made the mistake of having two children compensated for it by killing herself. The misogynist Canon of Literature can include these women because they can be perceived as incomplete women, as female men.

Still, I have to grit my teeth to criticise the either-books-or-babies doctrine, because it has given real, true comfort to women who could not or chose not to marry and have children, and saw themselves as 'having' books instead. But

---

[*] Alicia Ostriker, *Writing Like a Woman*, Michigan Poets on Poetry Series (Ann Arbor: University of Michigan Press, 1983).

[†] A particularly exhilarating discussion of this issue is the essay 'Writing and Motherhood' by Susan Rubin Suleiman, in *The (M)other Tongue: Essays in Feminist Psychoanalytic Interpretation*, edited by Garner, Kahane, and Springnether (Ithaca: Cornell University Press, 1985). Suleiman gives a short history of the nineteenth-century books-or-babies theory and its refinement in the twentieth century by such psychologists as Helene Deutsch, remarking that 'it took psychoanalysis to transform moral obligation into a psychological "law", equating the creative impulse with the procreative one and decreeing that she who has a child feels no need to write books.' Suleiman presents a critique of the feminist reversal of this theory (she who has a book feels no need to have children) and analyses current French feminist thinking on the relationship between writing and femininity/motherhood.

though the comfort may be real, I think the doctrine false. And I hear that falseness when a Dorothy Richardson tells us that other women can have children but nobody else can write her books. As if 'other women' could have had her children – as if books came from the uterus! That's just the flip side of the theory that books come from the scrotum. This final reduction of the notion of sublimation is endorsed by our chief macho dodo writer, who has announced that 'the one thing a writer needs to have is balls'. But he doesn't carry the theory of penile authorship to the extent of saying that if you 'get' a kid you can't 'get' a book and so fathers can't write. The analogy collapsed into identity, the you-can't-create-if-you-procreate myth, is applied to women only.

I've found I have to stop now and say clearly what I'm not saying. I'm not saying a writer ought to have children, I'm not saying a parent ought to be a writer, I'm not saying any woman ought to write books or have kids. Being a mother is one of the things a woman can do – like being a writer. It's a privilege. It's not an obligation, or a destiny. I'm talking about mothers who write because it is almost a taboo topic – because women have been told that they ought not to try to be both a mother and a writer because both the kids and the books will pay – because it can't be done – because it is unnatural.

This refusal to allow both creation and procreation to women is cruelly wasteful: not only has it impoverished our literature by banning the housewives, but it has caused unbearable personal pain and self-mutilation: Woolf obeying the wise doctors who said she must not bear a child; Plath who put glasses of milk by her kids' beds and then put her head in the oven.

A sacrifice, not of somebody else but of oneself, is demanded of women artists (while the Gauguin Pose demands of men artists only that they sacrifice others). I am proposing that this ban on a woman artist's full sexuality is harmful not only to the woman but to the art.

There is less censure now, and more support, for a woman who wants both to bring up a family and work as an artist. But it's a small degree of improvement. The difficulty of trying to be responsible, hour after hour day after day for maybe twenty years, for the well-being of children and the excellence of books, is immense: it involves an endless expense of energy and an impossible weighing of competing priorities. And we don't know much about the process, because writers who are mothers haven't talked much about their motherhood — for fear of boasting? for fear of being trapped in the Mom trap, discounted? — nor have they talked much about their writing as in any way connected with their parenting, since the heroic myth demands that the two jobs be considered utterly opposed and mutually destructive.

But we heard a hint of something else from Oliphant; and here (thanks, Tillie) is the painter Käthe Kollwitz:

> I am gradually approaching the period in my life when work comes first. When both the boys were away for Easter, I hardly did anything but work. Worked, slept, ate and went for short walks. But above all I worked.
>
> And yet I wonder whether the 'blessing' isn't missing from such work. No longer diverted by other emotions, I work the way a cow grazes.

That is marvellous — 'I work the way a cow grazes.' That is the best description of the 'professional' at work I know.

> Perhaps in reality I accomplish a little more. The hands work and work, and the head imagines it's producing God knows what,

and yet, formerly, when my working time was so wretchedly
limited, I was more productive, because I was more sensual;
I lived as a human being must live, passionately interested in
everything . . . Potency, potency is diminishing.[*]

This potency felt by a woman is a potency from which the
Hero-Artist has (and I choose my words carefully) cut
himself off, in an egoism that is ultimately sterile. But it is
a potency that has been denied by women as well as men,
and not just women eager to collude with misogyny.

Back in the seventies Nina Auerbach wrote that Jane
Austen was able to write because she had created around her
'a child-free space'. Germ-free I knew, odour-free I knew,
but child-free? And Austen? who wrote in the parlour, and
was a central figure to a lot of nieces and nephews? But I
tried to accept what Auerbach said, because although my
experience didn't fit it, I was, like many women, used to
feeling that my experience was faulty, not right – that it
was wrong. So I was probably wrong to keep on writing in
what was then a fully child-filled space. However, feminist
thinking evolved rapidly to a far more complex and realistic position, and I, stumbling along behind, have been
enabled by it to think a little for myself.

The greatest enabler for me was always, is always,
Virginia Woolf. And I quote now from the first draft of her
paper 'Professions for Women',[†] where she gives her great
image of a woman writing.

I figure her really in an attitude of contemplation, like a fisherwoman, sitting on the bank of a lake with her fishing rod held
over its water. Yes that is how I see her. She was not thinking;
she was not reasoning; she was not constructing a plot; she

[*] Käthe Kollwitz, diaries and letters, quoted in Olsen.

82

was letting her imagination down into the depths of her consciousness while she sat above holding on by a thin but quite
necessary thread of reason.

Now I interrupt to ask you to add one small element to
this scene. Let us imagine that a bit farther up the bank
of the lake sits a child, the fisherwoman's daughter. She's
about five, and she's making people out of sticks and mud
and telling stories with them. She's been told to be very
quiet please while Mama fishes, and she really is very
quiet except when she forgets and sings or asks questions;
and she watches in fascinated silence when the following
dramatic events take place. There sits our woman writing,
our fisherwoman, when –

suddenly there is a violent jerk; she feels the line race through
her fingers.
   The imagination has rushed away; it has taken to the depths;
it has sunk heaven knows where – into the dark pool of extraordinary experience. The reason has to cry 'Stop!', the novelist
has to pull on the line and haul the imagination to the surface.
The imagination comes to the top in a state of fury.
   Good heavens she cries – how dare you interfere with me
– how dare you pull me out with your wretched little fishing
line? And I – that is, the reason – have to reply, 'My dear you
were going altogether too far. Men would be shocked.' Calm
yourself I say, as she sits panting on the bank – panting with

† The talk, known in its revised form as 'Professions for Women'
and so titled in the Essays, was given on January 21, 1931, to the
London National Society for Women's Service, and can be found
complete with all deletions and alternate readings in Mitchell
Leaska's editing of Woolf's *The Pargiters* (London: The Hogarth
Press, 1978).

rage and disappointment. We have only got to wait fifty years
or so. In fifty years I shall be able to use all this very queer
knowledge that you are ready to bring me. But not now. You see
I go on, trying to calm her, I cannot make use of what you tell
me – about women's bodies for instance – their passions – and
so on, because the conventions are still very strong. If I were to
overcome the conventions I should need the courage of a hero,
and I am not a hero.

I doubt that a writer can be a hero. I doubt that a hero can be
a writer . . . Very well, says the imagination, dressing herself
up again in her petticoat and skirts, we will wait. We will wait
another fifty years. But it seems to me a pity.

It seems to me a pity. It seems to me a pity that more than
fifty years have passed and the conventions, though utterly
different, still exist to protect men from being shocked, still
admit only male experience of women's bodies, passions,
and existence. It seems to me a pity that so many women,
including myself, have accepted this denial of their own
experience and narrowed their perception to fit it, writing
as if their sexuality were limited to copulation, as if they
knew nothing about pregnancy, birth, nursing, mothering, puberty, menstruation, menopause, except what men
are willing to hear, nothing except what men are willing
to hear about housework, childwork, lifework, war, peace,
living and dying as experienced in the female body and
mind and imagination. 'Writing the body', as Woolf asked
and Hélène Cixous asks, is only the beginning. We have to
rewrite the world.

White writing, Cixous calls it, writing in milk, in
mother's milk. I like that image, because even among feminists, the woman writer has been more often considered
in her sexuality as a lover than in her sexuality as preg-

nant-bearing-nursing-childcaring. Mother still tends to get disappeared. And in losing the artist-mother we lose where there's a lot to gain. Alicia Ostriker thinks so. 'The advantage of motherhood for a woman artist,' she says – have you ever heard anybody say that before? the advantage of motherhood for an artist? –

> The advantage of motherhood for a woman artist is that it puts her in immediate and inescapable contact with the sources of life, death, beauty, growth, corruption . . . If the woman artist has been trained to believe that the activities of motherhood are trivial, tangential to the main issues of life, irrelevant to the great themes of literature, she should untrain herself. The training is misogynist, it protects and perpetuates systems of thought and feeling which prefer violence and death to love and birth, and it is a lie . . . 'We think back through our mothers, if we are women,' declares Woolf, but through whom can those who are themselves mothers . . . do their thinking? . . . we all need data, we need information, . . . the sort provided by poets, novelists, artists, from within. As our knowledge begins to accumulate, we can imagine what it would signify to all women, and men, to live in a culture where childbirth and mothering occupied the kind of position that sex and romantic love have occupied in literature and art for the last five hundred years, or . . . that warfare has occupied since literature began.*

My book *Always Coming Home* was a rash attempt to imagine such a world, where the Hero and the Warrior are a stage adolescents go through on their way to becoming responsible human beings, where the parent-child relationship is not forever viewed through the child's eyes but includes the reality of the mother's experience. The imagining was

* Ostriker, *Writing Like a Woman*.

difficult, and rewarding.

Here is a passage from a novel where what Woolf, Cixous and Ostriker ask for is happening, however casually and unpretentiously. In Margaret Drabble's *The Millstone*,[*] Rosamund, a young scholar and freelance writer, has a baby about eight months old, Octavia. They share a flat with a friend, Lydia, who's writing a novel. Rosamund is working away on a book review:

> I had just written and counted my first hundred words when I remembered Octavia; I could hear her making small happy noises . . . I was rather dismayed when I realized she was in Lydia's room and that I must have left the door open, for Lydia's room was always full of nasty objects like aspirins, safety razors and bottles of ink; I rushed along to rescue her and the sight that met my eyes when I opened the door was enough to make anyone quake. She had her back to the door and was sitting in the middle of the floor surrounded by a sea of torn, strewed, chewed paper. I stood there transfixed, watching the neat small back of her head and her thin stalk-like neck and flowery curls: suddenly she gave a great screech of delight and ripped another sheet of paper. 'Octavia,' I said in horror, and she started guiltily, and looked round at me with a charming deprecating smile: her mouth, I could see, was wedged full of wads of Lydia's new novel.
>
> I picked her up and fished the bits out and laid them carefully on the bedside table with what was left of the typescript; pages 70 to 123 seemed to have survived. The rest was in varying stages of dissolution: some pages were entire but badly crumpled, some were in large pieces, some in small pieces,

[*] Margaret Drabble, *The Millstone* (London: Weidenfeld and Nicolson Ltd, 1965).

and some, as I have said, were chewed up. The damage was not, in fact, as great as it appeared at first sight to be, for babies, though persistent, are not thorough: but at first sight it was frightful . . . In a way it was clearly the most awful thing for which I had ever been responsible, but as I watched Octavia crawl around the sitting room looking for more work to do, I almost wanted to laugh. It seemed so absurd, to have this small living extension of myself, so dangerous, so vulnerable, for whose injuries and crimes I alone had to suffer . . . It really was a terrible thing . . . and yet in comparison with Octavia being so sweet and so alive it did not seem so very terrible . . .

Confronted with the wreckage, Lydia is startled, but not deeply distressed:

. . . and that was it, except for the fact that Lydia really did have to rewrite two whole chapters as well as doing a lot of boring sellotaping, and when it came out it got bad reviews anyway. This did succeed in making Lydia angry.

I have seen Drabble's work dismissed with the usual list of patronising adjectives reserved for women who write as women, not imitation men. Let us not let her be disappeared. Her work is deeper than its bright surface. What is she talking about in this funny passage? Why does the girl-baby eat not her mother's manuscript but another woman's manuscript? Couldn't she at least have eaten a manuscript by a man? – no, no, that's not the point. The point, or part of it, is that babies eat manuscripts. They really do. The poem not written because the baby cried, the novel put aside because of a pregnancy, and so on. Babies eat books. But they spit out wads of them that can be taped back together; and they are only babies for a couple of years, while writers live for decades; and it is terrible, but not very terrible. The manuscript that got eaten was terrible; if you know Lydia you know the reviewers were right. And that's part of the point too – that the supreme value of art depends on other equally supreme values. But that subverts the hierarchy of values; 'men would be shocked . . .'

In Drabble's comedy of morals the absence of the Hero-Artist is a strong ethical statement. Nobody lives in a great isolation, nobody sacrifices human claims, nobody even scolds the baby. Nobody is going to put their head, or anybody else's head, into an oven: not the mother, not the writer, not the daughter – these three and one who, being women, do not separate creation and destruction into I *create/You are destroyed*, or vice versa. Who are responsible, take responsibility, for both the baby and the book.*

But I want now to turn from fiction to biography and from general to personal; I want to talk a bit about my mother, the writer.

Her maiden name was Theodora Kracaw; her first married name was Brown; her second married name, Kroeber, was the one she used on her books; her third married name was Quinn. This sort of many-namedness doesn't happen to men; it's inconvenient, and yet its very cumbersomeness reveals, perhaps, the being of a woman writer as not one simple thing – the author – but a multiple, complex process of being, with various responsibilities, one of which is to her writing.

Theodora put her personal responsibilities first – chronologically. She brought up and married off her four children before she started to write. She took up the pen, as they used to say – she had the most amazing left-handed scrawl – in her mid-fifties. I asked her once, years later, 'Did you want to write, and put it off intentionally, till you'd got rid of us?' And she laughed and said, 'Oh, no, I just wasn't ready.' Not an evasion or a dishonest answer, but not, I think, the whole answer.

She was born in 1897 in a wild Colorado mining town, and her mother boasted of having been born with the vote – in Wyoming, which ratified woman suffrage along with statehood – and rode a stallion men couldn't ride; but still, the Angel in the House was very active in those days, the one whose message is that a woman's needs come after everybody else's. And my mother really came pretty close to incarnating that Angel, whom Woolf called 'the woman men wish women to be'. Men fell in love with her – all men. Doctors, garage mechanics, professors, roach exterminators. Butchers saved sweetbreads for her. She was also, to her daughter, a demanding, approving, nurturing, good-natured, loving, lively mother – a first-rate mother. And then, getting on to sixty, she became a first-rate writer.

* My understanding of this issue has been much aided by Carol Gilligan's In a Different Voice (Cambridge: Harvard University Press, 1982), as well as by Jean Baker Miller's modestly revolutionary Toward a New Psychology of Women (Boston: Beacon Press, 1976). Gilligan's thesis, stated very roughly, is that our society brings up males to think and speak in terms of their rights, females in terms of their responsibilities, and that conventional psychologies have implicitly evaluated the 'male' image of a hierarchy of rights as 'superior' (hierarchically, of course) to the 'female' image of a network of mutual responsibilities. Hence a man finds it (relatively) easy to assert his 'right' to be free of relationships and dependents, à la Gauguin, while women are not granted and do not grant one another any such right, preferring to live as part of an intense and complex network in which freedom is arrived at, if at all, mutually. Coming at the matter from this angle, one can see why there are no or very few 'Great Artists' among women, when the 'Great Artist' is defined as inherently superior to and not responsible towards others.

She started out, as women so often do, by writing some books for children – not competing with men, you know, staying in the 'domestic sphere'. One of these, *A Green Christmas*, is a lovely book that ought to be in every six-year-old's stocking. Then she wrote a charming and romantic autobiographical novel – still on safe, 'womanly' ground. Next she ventured into Native American territory with *The Inland Whale*; and then she was asked to write the story of an Indian called Ishi, the only survivor of a people massacred by the North American pioneers, a serious and risky subject requiring a great deal of research, moral sensitivity, and organisational and narrative skill.

So she wrote it, the first bestseller, I believe, that University of California Press ever published. *Ishi* is still in print in many languages, still used, I think, in California schools, still deservedly beloved. It is a book entirely worthy of its subject, a book of very great honesty and power.

So, if she could write that in her sixties, what might she have written in her thirties? Maybe she really 'wasn't ready'. But maybe she listened to the wrong angel, and we might have had many more books from her. Would my brothers and I have suffered, have been cheated of anything, if she had been writing them? I think my aunt Betsy and the household help we had back then would have kept things going just fine. As for my father, I don't see how her writing could have hurt him or how her success could have threatened him. But I don't know. All I do know is that once she started writing (and it was while my father was alive, and they collaborated on a couple of things), she never stopped; she had found the work she loved.

Once, not long after my father's death, when *Ishi* was bringing her the validation of praise and success she very much needed, and while I was still getting every story I sent out rejected with monotonous regularity, she burst into tears over my latest rejection slip and tried to console me, saying that she wanted rewards and success for me, not for herself. And that was lovely, and I treasured her saying it then as I do now. That she didn't really mean it and I didn't really believe it made no difference. Of course she didn't want to sacrifice her achievement, her work, to me – why on earth should she? She shared what she could of it with me by sharing the pleasures and anguishes of writing, the intellectual excitement, the shoptalk – and that's all. No angelic altruism. When I began to publish, we shared that. And she wrote on; in her eighties she told me, without bitterness, 'I wish I had started sooner. Now there isn't time.' She was at work on a third novel when she died.

As for myself: I have flagrantly disobeyed the either-books-or-babies rule, having had three kids and written about twenty books, and thank God it wasn't the other way around. By the luck of race, class, money and health, I could manage the double-tightrope trick – and especially by the support of my partner. He is not my wife; but he brought to marriage an assumption of mutual aid as its daily basis, and on that basis you can get a lot of work done. Our division of labour was fairly conventional; I was in charge of house, cooking, the kids and novels, because I wanted to be, and he was in charge of being a professor, the car, the bills, and the garden, because he wanted to be. When the kids were babies I wrote at night; when they started school I wrote while they were at school; these days I write as a cow grazes. If I needed help he gave it without making it into a big favour, and – this is the central fact – he did not ever begrudge me the time I spent writing, or the blessing of my work.

That is the killer: the killing grudge, the envy, the jealousy, the spite that so often a man is allowed to hold, trained to hold, against anything a woman does that's not done in his service, for him, to feed his body, his comfort, his kids. A woman who tries to work against that grudge finds the blessing turned into a curse; she must rebel and go it alone, or fall silent in despair. Any artist must expect to work amid the total, rational indifference of everybody else to their work, for years, perhaps for life: but no artist can work well against daily, personal, vengeful resistance. And that's exactly what many women artists get from the people they love and live with.

I was spared all that. I was free – born free, lived free. And for years that personal freedom allowed me to ignore the degree to which my writing was controlled and constrained by judgements and assumptions which I thought were my own, but which were the internalised ideology of a male supremacist society. Even when subverting the conventions, I disguised my subversions from myself. It took me years to realise that I chose to work in such despised, marginal genres as science fiction, fantasy, young adult, precisely because they were excluded from critical, academic, canonical supervision, leaving the artist free; it took ten more years before I had the wits and guts to see and say that the exclusion of the genres from 'literature' is unjustified, unjustifiable, and a matter not of quality but of politics. So too in my choice of subjects: until the mid-seventies I wrote my fiction about heroic adventures, high-tech futures, men in the halls of power, men – men were the central characters, the women were peripheral, secondary. Why don't you write about women? my mother asked me. I don't know how, I said. A stupid answer, but an honest one. I did not know how to write about women – very few of us did – because I thought that what men had written about women was the truth, was the true way to write about women. And I couldn't.

My mother could not give me what I needed. When feminism began to reawaken, she hated it, called it 'those women's libbers'; but it was she who had steered me years and years before to what I would and did need, to Virginia Woolf. 'We think back through our mothers', and we have many mothers, those of the body and those of the soul. What I needed was what feminism, feminist literary theory and criticism and practice, had to give me. And I can hold it in my hands – not only *Three Guineas*, my treasure in the days of poverty, but now all the wealth of *The Norton Anthology of Literature by Women* and the reprint houses and the women's presses. Our mothers have been returned to us. This time, let's hang on to them.

And it is feminism that has empowered me to criticise not only my society and myself but – for a moment now – feminism itself. The books-or-babies myth is not only a misogynist hang-up, it can be a feminist one. Some of the women I respect most, writing for publications that I depend on for my sense of women's solidarity and hope, continue to declare that it is 'virtually impossible for a heterosexual woman to be a feminist', as if heterosexuality were heterosexism; and that social marginality, such as that of lesbian, childless, Black, or Native American women, 'appears to be necessary' to form the feminist. Applying these judgements to myself, and believing that as a woman writing at this point I have to be a feminist to be worth beans, I find myself, once again, excluded – disappeared.

The rationale of the exclusionists, as I understand it, is that the material privilege and social approbation our society grants the heterosexual wife, and particularly the mother, prevent her solidarity with less privileged women and insulate her from the kind of anger and the kind of ideas that lead to feminist action. There is truth in this; maybe it's true for a lot of women; I can oppose it only with my experience, which is that feminism has been a life-saving necessity to women trapped in the wife/mother 'role'. What do the privilege and approbation accorded the housewife-mother by our society in fact consist of? Being the object of infinite advertising? Being charged by psychologists with total answerability for children's mental well-being, and by the government with total answerability for children's welfare, while being regularly equated with apple pie by sentimental warmongers? As a social 'role', motherhood, for any woman I know, simply means that she does everything everybody else does plus bringing up the kids.

To push mothers back into 'private life', a mythological space invented by the patriarchy, on the theory that their acceptance of the 'role' of mother invalidates them for public, political, artistic responsibility, is to play Old Nobodaddy's game, by his rules, on his side.

In *Writing Beyond the Ending*, Du Plessis shows how women novelists write about the woman artist: they make her an ethical force, an activist trying 'to change the life in which she is also immersed'.* To have and bring up kids is to be about as immersed in life as one can be, but it does not always follow that one drowns. A lot of us can swim.

Again, whenever I give a version of this paper, somebody will pick up on this point and tell me that I'm supporting the Superwoman syndrome, saying that a woman should have kids write books be politically active and make perfect sushi. I am not saying that. We're all asked to be Superwoman; I'm not asking it, our society does that. All I can tell you is that I believe it's a lot easier to write books while bringing up kids than to bring up kids while work-

* Du Plessis, *Writing Beyond the Ending*.

ing nine to five plus housekeeping. But that is what our society, while sentimentalising over Mom and the Family, demands of most women – unless it refuses them any work at all and dumps them onto welfare and says, Bring up your kids on food stamps, Mom, we might want them for the army. Talk about superwomen, those are the super-women. Those are the mothers up against the wall. Those are the marginal women, without either privacy or pub-licity; and it's because of them more than anyone else that the woman artist has a responsibility to 'try to change the life in which she is also immersed'.

And now I come back round to the bank of that lake, where the fisherwoman sits, our woman writer, who had to bring her imagination up short because it was getting too deeply immersed . . . The imagination dries herself off, still swearing under her breath, and buttons up her blouse, and comes to sit beside the little girl, the fisher-woman's daughter. 'Do you like books?' she says, and the child says, 'Oh, yes. When I was a baby I used to eat them, but now I can read. I can read all of Beatrix Potter by my-self, and when I grow up I'm going to write books, like Mama.'

'Are you going to wait till your children grow up, like Jo March and Theodora?'

'Oh, I don't think so,' says the child. 'I'll just go ahead and do it.'

'Then will you do as Harriet and Margaret and so many Harriets and Margarets have done and are still doing, and hassle through the prime of your life trying to do two full-time jobs that are incompatible with each other in pract-ice, however enriching their interplay may be both to the life and the art?'

'I don't know,' says the little girl. 'Do I have to?'

'Yes,' says the imagination, 'if you aren't rich and you

want kids.'

'I might want one or two,' says reason's child. 'But why do women have two jobs where men only have one? It isn't reasonable, is it?'

'Don't ask me!' snaps the imagination. 'I could think up a dozen better arrangements before breakfast! But who listens to me?'

The child sighs and watches her mother fishing. The fisherwoman, having forgotten that her line is no longer baited with the imagination, isn't catching anything, but she's enjoying the peaceful hour; and when the child speaks again she speaks softly. 'Tell me, Auntie. What is the one thing a writer has to have?'

'I'll tell you,' says the imagination. 'The one thing a writer has to have is not balls. Nor is it a child-free space. Nor is it even, speaking strictly on the evidence, a room of her own, though that is an amazing help, as is the goodwill and cooperation of the opposite sex, or at least the local, in-house representative of it. But she doesn't have to have that. The one thing a writer has to have is a pencil and some paper. That's enough, so long as she knows that she and she alone is in charge of that pencil, and responsible, she and she alone, for what it writes on the paper. In other words, that she's free. Not wholly free. Never wholly free. Maybe very partially. Maybe only in this one act, this sitting for a snatched moment being a woman writing, fishing the mind's lake. But in this, responsible; in this, autonomous; in this, free.'

'Auntie,' says the little girl, 'can I go fishing with you now?'

IN AND OUT
(1989)

From the quarter-inch-thick sheet of clay Jilly cut the oblong side walls and the square, peaked front and back walls. The texture of the clay was like butter when you're working sugar into it, or like boiled tongue. The clay-knife looked small in her fat fingers. It moved with a satisfying clean cut along right angles, exact, exacting, but not hard.

With the point of a paring knife she cut out a window low in a side wall, a small window high in the back wall, and the front door. She pinched and pressed a piece of clay to make it into a bit of uneven ground, the base on which she erected the walls one by one, joining the corners after running a water-dipped finger along each edge, and sealing the join the same way. The front wall went on last, fitting the edges of the side walls precisely. On the clay-daubed turntable now stood a roofless house three inches long and two inches high.

Her nieces had left some modelling clay, the oily kind, in a desk drawer. She had pinched out little animals, grotesque heads, from the greasy stuff and then mashed them back into the lump. She felt ashamed of playing like a child, of making ugly childish shapes. She hated sewing and got sick of reading. She kept thinking about some tiny houses she had seen once in Chinatown, made of brown clay, very delicate.

Kaye Forrest came in to sit with Mother one day, and after shopping at Hambleton's Jilly went by Bill Weisler's and asked him what kind of clay she could buy to just fool around with. Bill gave her an incredibly heavy little paper sack of dry dust. He gave her two clay-knives and an old turntable, and told her he'd bake whatever she made in his kiln, which he called 'kill', so long as she'd hollow out the thick pieces so that they wouldn't explode in the heat of the kiln. She kept trying to get away and he kept telling her how to mix the clay and how to make slip and what to use it for and that she should cover the clay and the pieces with damp cloths at night, and when she drove off he was yelling that if she wanted to try bringing pots up on his wheel she could come over any evening, which left her really wishing she was at the office where she could tell somebody. 'He said, "Come over and bring pots up on my wheel!"'

Mother wouldn't enjoy it. Men were allowed to make innuendo sort of jokes, but women did not understand them.

The idea of doing anything with old Bill Weisler was too dismaying to be very funny, actually, but it had been interesting to see the inside of his cabin, shelves and shelves with rows and rows of the bowls and pots and vases he sold in Portland, some raw and some baked and coloured. She knew he made a living as a potter, but she had never considered that that meant he lived there making pots, his hands in clay all day long, all night too, maybe.

She spun the table slowly, checking the walls for fit and verticality, admiring the view of the inside through the little oblong of the doorway.

Bringing the rolled-out slab round again, she measured off the length of the house and added a half inch for eaves, estimated the width with a margin for error, marked off the oblong, and cut out the roof. She ruled a line down the centre where the ridgepole would go, and then with an old fork and her thumbnail scored the surface of the clay with scratches to look like straw. She lifted the roof on a spatula and laid it on the walls. It fit, overhanging only a little too far on the sides. She took it off and trimmed the edges, raking them with the fork to look more like straw, then wet the surfaces where roof would rest on wall, added a little slip to seal the joins, and replaced the roof, pressing it gently down on the house. Now when she looked in through the doorway she saw light entering the house only through the windows. The house had an inside, a dim, eerie place she could peer into with her enormous eye but could not enter, even though she had made it.

She began to cut toothpicks of clay for the window- and door-frames. The work went well, easily, because she knew what she was doing. Her first house, squat and sorry, sat drying up on the bookshelf. With it were three improving versions, a small village of some very primitive tribe. But this one was coming out right. Almost like the ones in Chinatown.

She had been thinking, and the thought came back like the turntable coming round, that it was hard, or anyway she found it hard, to realise that what you did was usually just done once. Once and for all. That doing something wasn't just a kind of practice for something that would keep happening, but was what would happen, was what happened. You didn't get to practise.

Of course, there was all the stuff that needed doing over every day, housework, office work, old Bill's pots; but you treated that like it didn't matter, even when it was all you knew how to do well, and kept saving yourself up for the important things, and then when you did them you didn't know how. Like when the group of secretaries met to plan meetings to talk about women in the city government, and the meeting had been so terrific, people saying things they didn't even know they thought, and ideas coming up, and nobody pushing each other around. And then Jetz's exec sec told the women in her office that they couldn't go, and the group never met again. They had just been getting ready for the real meeting and they had had it, it was done. Why was it so hard to see while it was happening that that was what was happening? Even a marriage. About the time she grew up enough to realise that marriage was what she and David were doing, he had started wanting out. Maybe because he'd realised it, too. Who knows? Even just going to Chinatown. Not a tour to China or something like that you knew would be once in a lifetime, but just a shopping trip in Chinatown, and you saw some little clay houses, but you didn't buy them, you said, 'I'll get a couple of those when I come back.' And then it's years later and if you did go back they wouldn't be there. There might not be the same shops even.

So the thing about what she was doing, even if it was stupid, at least she'd practised it, and this time she was doing it right.

She was fitting the tiny frame around the doorway when her mother came through the room.

Jilly looked around and said, 'Hi!' She didn't want to look around or speak, but she had no excuse, she wasn't working, she was playing making toy houses. Nothing she did could be anything but playing, compared to what her mother was doing. She was walking from her bedroom, past the bathroom, through Jilly's room, to the sun-room at the back of the house. She wore the kimono Jilly had bought her in a second-hand store in Portland, embroidered in jade and apricot and gold, silly gorgeous silks over the thin and swollen places. She stopped in the doorway to the sun-room and said, 'The sun's got around back here now.'

Jilly bent over the turntable and made a cheerful sound. She heard her mother go on after a minute into the sun-room. There she would play at reading the newspaper, which Jilly had left for her by the armchair under the south windows. There she would play at sitting in the sun. But all the time she was working herself to death.

Since the last treatment she had not been outside. She did not cook or clean or crochet or play bridge or any of the things she had practised for a long time. She had been practising walking even longer, and she still did that. She could walk down the little hall to the bathroom by herself, and all the way to the sun-room. Jilly's father had closed in the south-facing back porch when he bought the house for their retirement home five years ago. He had had it roofed, put in windows and louvers and miniblinds, got it all fixed up 'so your mother can get the sun without the wind'. Then he had gone out into the front garden and taken hold of a hoe handle and thrown it from him with a shout, flinging his arms wide, and died – right then, right there, without any practice at all.

The garden he had started to put in stayed the way it was. When Ernest brought the girls for Thanksgiving he would prune the hydrangeas and cut back the laurel hedge. Jilly sometimes spent an hour on a weekend weeding around the roses, enjoying it and always sure she would do more next weekend. Now that she was staying here she hardly ever went into the garden, because Mother never did. Mother never had gone down to the beach even when she was well. She did not like the wind. And there were insects outside.

Last spring, when it was only in the lymph nodes, one of the doctors has recommended a book about imagination therapy, and Jilly had got it and read it aloud to her. The book told her to imagine armies of Helper Cells and Hero Cells winning the war. 'I thought about that army, like it said,' she told Jilly in the morning in her soft, flat voice. 'There was a whole lot of them. With wings. Sort of transparent.'

'Like angels?'

'No', her mother said. 'They were like those winged ant things, the whitish ones. They were crawling all over inside. Inside me.'

At first the radio played just what Kaye liked, Willie and Don and Emmy Lou, but then there were four or five songs in a row that were about bodies, your warm and tender body, they said, the word body with a kind of thick sound to it, and then love, of course, with that same thick back-of-the-throat sound, I luhrv yer buhrdy, so she finally turned it off. If they meant sex when they said love, fine, nobody knows what love means anyhow. But when the word for what you made love to was the same as for a corpse it sounded like it didn't matter whether the body was alive or dead. She sponged the counter clean, ran the disposal, wiped out the sink, rinsed the sponges, checked around with a glance, gathered up the sections of the newspaper Jack had left on the breakfast table, put them on the coffee table in the front room, and went into the empty room. The guest room.

Its windows faced east and were full of sunlight, which showed all the winter's salty, streaky grime on the glass. I can wash the windows, Kaye thought, but immediately postponed the reprieve, making it into a reward. After. She could wash the windows after.

Nothing was really dirty or even very dusty; nothing was disordered in the bright little room. But it had been eighteen months. It was time she could clean it like the rest of the house. It had been two months. Since she had dusted. At least two months. At Christmas, before Christmas. Four months. It was time. Things have their seasons. If Jack's niece really came for Easter she would have this room, the guest room. It would be her room. Karen's room. That was as it should be, people lived in rooms and left them and the rooms were still there. They were called Sarah's room, Karen's room, but they were the same place. That had to do with love. That had to do with why it bothered her when they sang about love as if they knew what it was, as if love meant anything in words at all.

Jack knew that. He never said 'I love you' except when he thought he had to, and it embarrassed both of them when he did. She never said it at all. On Valentine's Day she put a valentine under his dinner plate. Red paper hearts, white paper lace, cartoon cupids, that was 'I love you'. That was fine. All right. But there was this other thing that was dark, that had nothing to do with talking, with words, that was here, now, in this room – that was this room in her and her in this room, the heaviness of her body, her living body in the absence of the dead. That was what they didn't sing about.

The bed should be aired. It had stood made up all winter, getting damp. She turned her back on the bad place, the shelves, and whipped the spread and blankets off the bed. Different blankets, she had given the others away. She pulled out and bundled up the sheets, took the mattress pad off and pushed the bed out a bit so that the sunlight would fall right across it. She took the sheets to the laundry basket on the back porch and hung the mattress pad on the lines there to air out. When she came back into the room, it looked like a motel room being cleaned, torn apart, unfamiliar. She turned at once to the shelves.

She moved Sarah's toys down onto the bureau so that she could dust the shelves. She handled the things firmly. They weren't really toys. There were the two plastic horses, the Thoroughbred and the Appaloosa. When they were seven or eight Jannine would bring her horses over and the two girls would play, down in the dunes, all afternoon. Sarah had kept the horses because they were pretty. They weren't toys any more, just pretty things she had liked. They had a right to stay there. It was all right. Things that weren't pretty, that had only been toys or only been useful, not loved, those it wouldn't have been right to keep. Jack had wanted to leave everything, keep everything. He had never forgiven her for giving away the toys, the clothes, the blankets. Even though he knew they couldn't keep them, and never spoke of it, and probably never thought about it, he had never forgiven her. People never forgave you for doing what had to be done that they wouldn't do themselves. Like those caste people in India, little dark stick-people on the TV, who looked after dirty clothes and garbage and corpses. Nobody would touch them. If you got rid of dirt you got dirty. It made sense. Jack didn't want anything in the room to be treated like dirt, to be got rid of. But it had to be. Somebody had to.

The pretty, oh, the pretty little tiger, she had forgotten it – made of red and yellow and black silk and tiny mirrors sewed in – from somewhere in India, was that why she had thought about India? – Jannine had given it to Sarah the last Christmas. With its silly cat smile, and mirrors down its striped sides. She put it down. She put it down. Beside the bookend, the sailing ship.

Jack made that before they were married. What fine work he used to do, inlay and pierced carving. Maybe when he retired he would go back to work like that. Maybe she could ask him then to make that piece he had designed years ago, in the other house. He would have the designs somewhere, he never threw anything away. A chest with a design of sea creatures on the lid in inlay, and seahorses at the corners holding it up. In the drawing you thought the chest had scalloped corners, and then you saw the seahorses standing on their curled tails. Bearing that in mind, she dusted the books and set them back behind the bookend and turned at last to the easy parts of the room.

The sunlight in the windows was so bright it darkened her eyes and she felt cold through, as if the room itself were cold, and dark, and very close, too close. The telephone in the kitchen rang, and she ran.

'Have to go up to Astoria,' Jack said. His husky, grumbling voice was full of his physical presence, his body, thick, firm, solid, defenceless. 'They sent the wrong insulation. Fuck it up every time.' He grumbled but forgave them. He never looked for anything to go smoothly, only to go along smoothly himself, ducking under, as he said, letting the shit fly overhead. Lessons of Nam, he said. 'Anything you want there?'

'I don't think so.'

'So I won't be back for lunch.'

'Well, get something to eat there, then.'

'OK.'

'Wait. Listen, where's the stepladder.'

'At the shop.'

'Oh.'

'I'll bring it home this evening. Used it fixing that moulding on the Martins' house. What d'you need it for?'

'Washing windows.'

105

'Outside? Leave that to me.'

'I can do the ones I can reach, anyhow.'

'OK. See you.'

'Take care.'

She would eat lunch early, then, and go over and sit with Joyce Dant. She called the Dants. Jilly's voice, too, was full of her body, warm, fat and soft, a bit breathless like a girl and yet retreating, not touching, not quite meeting you. 'Oh, hi, Kaye!' she said warmly, but Kaye felt like she was intruding.

'I'd like to come visit with Joyce this afternoon. If you have errands or anything, it's a pretty day to be out in.'

'Oh, that's really nice of you, Kaye. I don't think there's anything we need.'

'Well, I'll just come and sit a bit.' She could feel Jilly's resistance. You always resisted, you felt like you had to be there, you had to be there. Somebody had to feel that way.

'I'll be over about two,' Kaye said, and hung up. She knew Jilly couldn't argue with her. She knew her own authority, and its source.

Jilly was cutting posts for the roofed veranda she had decided to build on the front of her house, when her mother spoke from the sun room. 'It's lovely and warm in here,' she said.

Jilly answered loudly, 'Yes! I bet it is!' But she would not go in there. This was her hour. Her one hour in the whole day. She went on cutting the shred of clay. All the rest of the time she was there to do what there was to do, but this one hour she kept back, kept out, to make stupid little imitation Chinatown mud houses. It wasn't fair of her mother to try to claim this one piece of time, too. Everything else was hers. This was Jilly's time, playtime, fat mud Jilly making mud pies.

Her mother spoke again, indistinctly responding to something she was reading in the paper. Jilly did not ask 'What?' She pretended she had not heard. She could not stop listening. She never stopped listening except some nights when she fell into a sleep like stone and woke appalled at her sleep, her absence, while her mother lay struggling at her work which the drugs were supposed to make easy. Was long the same as easy? But now, just now, her mother did not really need her, she was only jealous.

The pages of the newspaper rustled, turning. Relieved, Jilly shifted her weight on the uncomfortable chair and went on working on the veranda roof. It was going to have to have a thicker beam running between the posts to keep it from sagging. Once she got that right, the roofed veranda made the house complete. The glimpse of the interior through the doorway was more charming and mysterious than ever. Though if you were an inch high and could actually go inside, you'd be in a single room whose floor and walls and roof were nothing but cold, damp, bare clay. It would be horrible. It's the inside seen from the outside, Jilly thought, bringing the turntable round, that always seems so mysterious and wonderful, and that's why—

Her mother spoke again. She wasn't talking to the paper, this was a different voice. Alone in the sun-flooded room, not fully awake, since the new higher dosage caused half-states and twilights of consciousness, she was thinking aloud, her mind was working on some question or problem, working something out. She said a few more words in a murmur and then clearly, in her small, flat voice, 'All right. That's it, then. All right.'

Jilly knew what she had asked and answered. Why had her daughter not come at her invitation, when she said it was warm and lovely here? Because she could no longer invite. She couldn't say, 'Come in.' She could only demand, 'Come here!' or beg, 'Come to me?' And her daughter did not want to come. All right.

But it wasn't true. Her daughter wanted to come but couldn't. She couldn't go into that room. She could only look in from the outside.

She set the finished house up on the shelf to dry. She dampened the clayey cloth and laid it over the unshaped lump. Her hands were daubed and coated greyish-white, and she went to wash them. The telephone rang, and as she turned to it she called to her mother, 'I'll be there in just a moment.'

Joyce wanted to watch one of the afternoon soaps. She told Kaye what the episode was going to be about, but as soon as it started she fell asleep. Kaye knitted. The afternoon sun was on the windows of the bedroom, but the miniblinds were closed tight, shutting out the sunlight and the sea. Kaye wondered, if she were dying, would she want to be in a room with a sea view. She wondered if Joyce looked out at the sea.

Joyce lay like sticks and lumps in the bed, her face half turned away.

Kaye knew little of her. She and her husband had moved here five years ago, and he had died that first year. She had stayed, quiet, flat-talking. She was from the East somewhere, Ohio, maybe. She had a way of being aggrieved, down on things, but she had a funny streak, a kind of prim wryness. She wore brown and navy skirts, tan cardigans. Jilly would have given her the beautiful, brilliant housecoat that lay across the foot of the bed. Jilly was a good daughter, coming over from Portland every weekend when Joyce was newly widowed, and now staying here full time. She had a job at City Hall that she must have given up or got leave from. It would be hard to ask her about it. Jilly was much more open and easy than her mother, but she held back, too. Kaye had told her to go out and have a walk on the beach, it was so beautiful out, but Jilly said she wanted a nap and was in her room now, the blinds drawn. The three of them shut indoors with the windows covered, and outside the April sunlight pouring down on shore and sea, and the wind as warm as summer.

'Where's Jilly?'

'Having a nap,' Kaye said in a murmur, knowing Joyce was less than half awake.

'She never comes.'

'Oh, now, now,' Kaye soothed, cajoling, dismissing. Joyce slipped further back into sleep. Did she 'love' her daughter? Kaye watched her bony, swollen hand lying on the blanket. Can you love people when you're dying?

Why did you have me if this was going to happen?

But she had only been fourteen.

Jilly thumped around in the hall and the bathroom, and came to the doorway of the room, flushed from sleep, a big rose-and-golden woman. Soft and tender. 'How's about a cup of tea, you two?' she said aloud.

Joyce did not answer. Probably her sleeping and waking were not much affected by anything outside her own body now. Her body, the sticks and lumps under the covering. 'A rag, a bone and a hank of hair,' Kaye's father used to sing, teasing Mother, when she'd bought a new dress or got a perm and a rinse. And so they all were, that or a little dust in the sea, the soft and tender bodies, nothing much to sing about, but so you dyed and curled your hair, to look pretty.

Jilly came back with a tray. Joyce roused up. They drank tea together.

'Well, I'd better go home and wash my windows,' Kaye said. 'I've dodged it long enough.'

109

'Sun coming out makes you see how dirty they've got,' said Joyce.

'Awful. And I can't do the outside of most of them till Jack brings the stepladder back. But I can do the insides, and finish cleaning Sarah's room. Jack's niece will be with us Easter week, did I tell you? Karen Jones. She's at the health sciences college in town.'

'Newspaper's better than paper towels. For windows. Something in the printing, in the ink.' Joyce shifted in the bed and breathed heavily. She looked directly at Kaye, one brief gaze, full of hate. Don't come here with your dead daughter!

'So, I'd better be off. Anything I can do for either of you? You know, if you need anything from Astoria, Jack's up there two or three times a week.'

'Oh, no, we're just fine.'

She went with Kaye through the front room and they stood a moment, Kaye outside on the porch, Jilly in the doorway, holding the door open. The light, sweet, moving air touched them. Kaye put a hand for a moment on Jilly's arm. She saw the nails of Jilly's hand rimmed as if she had been digging in clay. She only touched her, she did not embrace her, for Jilly did not expect to be embraced, and that made it hard, even for a mother who wanted to hold her daughter. 'It's hard, Jilly,' Kaye said.

'Hard work', Jilly said, smiling, already turning to go back inside.

TEXTS
(1990)

Messages came, Johanna thought, usually years too late, or years before one could crack their code or had even learned the language they were in. Yet they came increasingly often and were so urgent, so compelling in their demand that she read them, that she do something, as to force her at last to take refuge from them. She rented, for the month of January, a little house with no telephone in a seaside town that had no mail delivery. She had stayed in Klatsand several times in summer; winter, as she had hoped, was even quieter than summer. A whole day would go by without her hearing or even speaking a word. She did not buy the paper or turn on the television, and the one morning she thought she ought to find some news on the radio she got a programme in Finnish from Astoria. But the messages still came. Words were everywhere.

Literate clothing was no real problem. She remembered the first print dress she had ever seen, years ago, a genuine print dress with typography involved in the design – green on white, suitcases and hibiscus and the names *Riviera* and *Capri* and *Paris* occurring rather blobbily from shoulder seam to hem, sometimes right side up, sometimes upside

down. Then it had been, as the saleswoman said, very unusual. Now it was hard to find a T-shirt that did not urge
political action, or quote lengthily from a dead physicist,
or at least mention the town it was for sale in. All this she
had coped with, she had even worn. But too many things
were becoming legible.

She had noticed in earlier years that the lines of foam
left by waves on the sand after stormy weather lay sometimes in curves that looked like handwriting, cursive lines
broken by spaces, as if in words, but it was not until she
had been alone for over a fortnight and had walked many
times down to Wreck Point and back that she found she
could read the writing. It was a mild day, nearly windless,
so that she did not have to march briskly but could mosey
along between the foam-lines and the water's edge where
the sand reflected the sky. Every now and then a quiet winter breaker driving up and up the beach would drive her
and a few gulls ahead of it onto the drier sand, then as
the wave receded she and the gulls would follow it back.
There was not another soul on the long beach. The sand
lay as firm and even as a pad of pale brown paper, and on
it a recent wave at its high mark had left a complicated
series of curves and bits of foam. The ribbons and loops
and lengths of white looked so much like handwriting in
chalk that she stopped, the way she would stop, half willingly, to read what people scratched in the sand in summer.
Usually it was 'Jason + Karen' or paired initials in a heart;
once, mysteriously and memorably, three initials and the
dates 1973-1984, the only such inscription that spoke of
a promise not made but broken. Whatever those eleven
years had been, the length of a marriage? A child's life?
They were gone, and the letters and numbers also were
gone when she came back by where they had been, with
the tide rising. She had wondered then if the person who

112

wrote them had written them to be erased. But these foam words lying on the brown sand now had been written by the erasing sea itself. If she could read them they might tell her a wisdom a good deal deeper and bitterer than she could possibly swallow. Do I want to know what the sea writes? She thought, but at the same time she was already reading the foam, which though in vaguely cuneiform blobs rather than letters of any alphabet was perfectly legible as she walked along beside it. 'Yes,' it read, 'esse hes hetu tokye to' ossusess ekyes. Seham hute' u.' (When she wrote it down later she used the apostrophe to represent a kind of stop or click like the last sound in 'Yep!') As she read it over, backing up some yards to do so, it continued to say the same thing, so she walked up and down it several times and memorised it. Presently, as bubbles burst and the blobs began to shrink, it changed here and there to read, 'Yes e hes etu kye to' ossusess kye. ham te u.' She felt that this was not significant change but mere loss, and kept the original text in mind. The water of the foam sank into the sand and the bubbles dried away till the marks and lines lessened into a faint lacework of dots and scraps, half legible. It looked enough like delicate bits of fancywork that she wondered if one could also read lace or crochet.

When she got home she wrote down the foam words so that she would not have to keep repeating them to remember them, and then she looked at the machine-made Quaker lace tablecloth on the little round dining table. It was not hard to read but was, as one might expect, rather dull. She made out the first line inside the border as 'pith wot pith wot pith wot' interminably, with a 'dub' every thirty stitches where the border pattern interrupted.

But the lace collar she had picked up at a second-hand clothing store in Portland was a different matter entirely. It was handmade, handwritten. The script was small and very even. Like the Spencerian hand she had been taught fifty years ago in the first grade, it was ornate but surprisingly easy to read. 'My soul must go,' was the border, repeated many times, 'my soul must go, my soul must go,' and the fragile webs leading inward read, 'sister, sister, sister, light the light'. And she did not know what she was to do, or how she was to do it.

INTRODUCTING MYSELF
(1992)

Written in the early nineties as a performance piece.

I am a man. Now you may think I've made some kind of silly mistake about gender, or maybe that I'm trying to fool you, because my first name ends in a, and I own three bras, and I've been pregnant five times, and other things like that that you might have noticed, little details. But details don't matter. If we have anything to learn from politicians it's that details don't matter. I am a man, and I want you to believe and accept this as a fact, just as I did for many years.

You see, when I was growing up at the time of the Wars of the Medes and Persians and when I went to college just after the Hundred Years War and when I was bringing up my children during the Korean, Cold and Vietnam Wars, there were no women. Women are a very recent invention. I predate the invention of women by decades. Well, if you insist on pedantic accuracy, women have been invented several times in widely varying localities, but the inventors just didn't know how to sell the product. Their distribution techniques were rudimentary and their market research was nil, and so of course the concept just didn't get off the ground. Even with a genius behind it an invention has to find its market, and it seemed like for a long time the idea of women just didn't make it to the bottom line. Models like the Austen and the Brontë were too complicated, and people just laughed at the Suffragette, and the Woolf was way too far ahead of its time.

So when I was born, there actually were only men. People were men. They all had one pronoun, his pronoun; so that's who I am. I am the generic he, as in, 'If anybody needs an abortion he will have to go to another state,' or 'A writer knows which side his bread is buttered on.' That's me, the writer, him. I am a man.

Not maybe a first-rate man. I'm perfectly willing to admit that I may be in fact a kind of second-rate or imitation man, a Pretend-a-Him. As a him, I am to a genuine male him as a microwaved fish stick is to a whole grilled Chinook salmon. I mean, after all, can I inseminate? Can I belong to the Bohemian Club? Can I run General Motors? Theoretically I can, but you know where theory gets us. Not to the top of General Motors, and on the day when a Radcliffe woman is president of Harvard University you wake me up and tell me, will you? Only you won't have to, because there aren't any more Radcliffe women; they were found to be unnecessary and abolished. And then, I can't write my name with pee in the snow, or it would be awfully laborious if I did. I can't shoot my wife and children and some neighbours and then myself. Oh to tell you the truth I can't even drive. I never got my licence. I chickened out. I take the bus. That is terrible. I admit it, I am actually a very poor imitation or substitute man, and you could see it when I tried to wear those army surplus clothes with ammunition pockets that were trendy and I looked like a hen in a pillowcase. I am shaped wrong. People are supposed to be lean. You can't be too thin, everybody says so, especially anorexics. People are supposed to be lean and taut, because that's how men generally are, lean and taut, or anyhow that's how a lot of men start out and some of them even stay that way. And men are people, people are men, that has been well established, and so people, real people, the right kind of people, are lean. But I'm really lousy at being people, because I'm not lean at all but sort of podgy, with actual fat places. I am untaut. And then, people are supposed to be tough. Tough is good. But I've never been tough. I'm sort of soft and actually sort of tender. Like a good steak. Or like Chinook salmon, which isn't lean and tough but very rich and tender. But then salmon aren't people, or anyhow we have been told that they aren't, in recent years. We have been told that there is only one kind of people and they are men. And I think it is very important that we all believe that. It certainly is important to the men.

What it comes down to, I guess, is that I am just not manly. Like Ernest Hemingway was manly. The beard and the guns and the wives and the little short sentences. I do try. I have this sort of beardoid thing that keeps trying to grow, nine or ten hairs on my chin, sometimes even more; but what do I do with the hairs? I tweak them out. Would a man do that? Men don't tweak. Men shave. Anyhow white men shave, being hairy, and I have even less choice about being white or not than I do about being a man or not. I am white whether I like being white or not. The doctors can do nothing for me. But I do my best not to be white, I guess, under the circumstances, since I don't shave. I tweak. But it doesn't mean anything because I don't really have a real beard that amounts to anything. And I don't have a gun and I don't have even one wife and my sentences tend to go on and on and on, with all this syntax in them. Ernest Hemingway would have died rather than have syntax. Or semicolons. I use a whole lot of half-assed semicolons; there was one of them just now; that was a semicolon after 'semicolons', and another one after 'now'.

And another thing. Ernest Hemingway would have died rather than get old. And he did. He shot himself. A short sentence. Anything rather than a long sentence, a life sentence. Death sentences are short and very, very manly. Life sentences aren't. They go on and on, all full of syntax and qualifying clauses and confusing references and getting old. And that brings up the real proof of what a mess I have made of being a man: I am not even young. Just about the time they finally started inventing women, I started getting old. And I went right on doing it. Shamelessly. I have allowed myself to get old and haven't done one single thing about it, with a gun or anything.

What I mean is, if I had any real self-respect wouldn't I at least have had a face-lift or some liposuction? Although liposuction sounds to me like what they do a lot of on TV when they are young or youngish, though not when they are old, and when one of them is a man and the other a woman, though not under any other circumstances. What they do is, this young or youngish man and woman take hold of each other and slide their hands around on each other and then they perform liposuction. You are supposed to watch them while they do it. They move their heads around and flatten out their mouth and nose on the other person's mouth and nose and open their mouths in different ways, and you are supposed to feel sort of hot or wet or something as you watch. What I feel is like I'm watching two people doing liposuction, and this is why they finally invented women? Surely not.

As a matter of fact I think sex is even more boring as a spectator sport than all the other spectator sports, even baseball. If I am required to watch a sport instead of doing it, I'll take show jumping. The horses are really good-looking. The people who ride them are mostly these sort of nazis, but like all nazis they are only as powerful and successful as the horse they are riding, and it is after all the horse who decides whether to jump that five-barred gate or stop short and let the nazi fall off over its neck. Only usually the horse doesn't remember it has the option. Horses aren't awfully bright. But in any case, show jumping and sex have a good deal in common, though you usually can only get show jumping on American TV if you can pick up a Canadian channel, which is not true of sex. Given the option, though I often forget that I have an option, I certainly would *watch* show jumping and *do* sex. Never the other way round. But I'm too old now for show jumping, and as for sex, who knows? I do; you don't.

Of course golden oldies are supposed to jump from bed to bed these days just like the horses jumping the five-barred gates, bounce, bounce, bounce, but a good deal of this super sex at seventy business seems to be theory again, like the woman CEO of General Motors and the woman president of Harvard. Theory is invented mostly to reassure people in their forties, that is men, who are worried. That is why we had Karl Marx, and why we still have economists, though we seem to have lost Karl Marx. As such, theory is dandy. As for practice, or praxis as the Marxists used to call it apparently because they liked *x*'s, you wait till you are sixty or seventy and then you can tell me about your sexual practice, or praxis, if you want to, though I make no promises that I will listen, and if I do listen I will probably be extremely bored and start looking for some show jumping on the TV. In any case you are not going to hear anything from me about my sexual practice or praxis, then, now, or ever.

But all that aside, here I am, old, when I wrote this I was sixty years old, 'a sixty-year-old smiling public man,'

119

as Yeats said, but then, he *was* a man. And now I am over seventy. And it's all my own fault. I get born before they invent women, and I live all these decades trying so hard to be a good man that I forget all about staying young, and so I didn't. And my tenses get all mixed up. I just am young and then all of a sudden I was sixty and maybe eighty, and what next?

Not a whole lot.

I keep thinking there must have been something that a real man could have done about it. Something short of guns, but more effective than Oil of Olay. But I failed. I did nothing. I absolutely failed to stay young. And then I look back on all my strenuous efforts, because I really did try, I tried hard to be a man, to be a good man, and I see how I failed at that. I am at best a bad man. An imitation phoney second-rate him with a ten-hair beard and semi-colons. And I wonder what was the use. Sometimes I think I might just as well give the whole thing up. Sometimes I think I might just as well exercise my option, stop short in front of the five-barred gate, and let the nazi fall off onto his head. If I'm no good at pretending to be a man and no good at being young, I might just as well start pretending that I am an old woman. I am not sure that anybody has invented old women yet; but it might be worth trying.

OFF THE PAGE: LOUD COWS, A TALK AND A POEM ABOUT READING ALOUD (1992)

'Off the Page' was a talk for a conference on women and language held by graduate students of the Department of Linguistics at the University of California in Berkeley, in April 1998. In getting it ready for this book, I didn't change the informality of the language, since the piece not only is about reading aloud to a live audience but was written for performance. The audience was by no means all women, but they were more receptive to uncomforting remarks about gender equality than most academic groups. I have performed the poem 'Loud Cows' at that meeting, in New York, and elsewhere, and it appears as a frontispiece in The Ethnography of Reading, edited by Jonathan Boyarin.

What happened to stories and poems after the invention of printing is a strange and terrible thing. Literature lost its voice. Except on the stage, it was silenced. Gutenberg muzzled us.

By the time I got born the silence of literature was considered an essential virtue and a sign of civilisation. Nannies and grannies told stories aloud to babies, and 'primitive' peoples spoke their poems, poor illiterate jerks, but the real stuff, literature, was literally letters, letterpress, little black noiseless marks on paper. And libraries were temples of the goddess of silence attended by vigilant priestesses going *Shhhh*.

If you listen to the first Caedmon tape of poets reading, which was a landmark, you'll hear T.S. Eliot going *adduh, adduh* in this dull grey mutter, and Elizabeth Bishop going *gnengnengne* in a low flat whine. They were good poets who'd been taught poetry was to be seen not heard, and thought the music in their verse should be a secret between the poet and the reader – like the music that people who know how to read music hear when they read a score. Nobody was playing the music of poetry out loud.

Until Dylan Thomas. You know the Caedmon tape of him reading at Columbia in 1952? I was there at that reading, and you can hear me – in the passionate silence of the audience listening to that passionate voice. Not a conspiracy of silence, but a participatory silence, a community collaboration in letting him let the word loose aloud. I left that reading two feet above the ground, and it changed my understanding of the art forever.

So then there were the Beat poets, all posing and using and screwed up by testosterone, but at least audible, and Ginsberg's 'Howl', which from the title on is a true performance piece that will not lie down quietly on the paper and be good. And ever since then, our poets have been noisy. Now God knows there are too many open-mike readings in the world; but better drivel at an open mike than silence from a closed mouth. And we have the voices of all recent poets on tape, so we can hear their word on their breath, with their heartbeat in it. Whereas of the greatest English writer of the twentieth century we have one tiny BBC recording: about ninety seconds of Virginia Woolf's voice reading a little essay. But in it you hear an invaluable hint of the rhythm that she said was where all the words began for her, the mysterious rhythm of her own voice.

It wasn't till the seventies, I think, that publishers realised they could sell more books by sending the author to two hundred cities in eight days to sign them – and then realised that people like not only to see the author sit and grin and write its name, but also to hear the author stand up and read its story. So now you here in Berkeley have Black Oak and Cody's, and we in Portland have Powell's and the Looking Glass, and Seattle has Elliott Bay Books running two readings a day every day of the week, and people come. They come to be read to. Some of them want books signed and some of them want to ask weird questions, but most of them want to be read to. To hear the word.

One reason I think this is a restoration of an essential function of literature is that it is reciprocal: a social act. The audience is part of the performance. A lecture isn't reciprocal, it's a talking-to. There were professors at Harvard when I was there who would give you a C if you *breathed* during a lecture. But the hush during a performance is alive and responsive, as at the theatre. Nothing kills a play like a dead audience. This response is recognised and called for in all oral literatures. Zunis listening to a narrative recital say a word, *eeso*, meaning yes, OK, about once a minute and whenever appropriate. In oral cultures generally, kids are taught to make these soft response-noises; if they don't, it's assumed they weren't listening and they're sent out in disgrace. Any Baptist preacher who doesn't hear Yes Lord! and Amen! pretty often knows he's lost the congregation. In poetry readings, big groups or small, the convention is mostly a little soft groan or hahh at a striking line or at the end. In prose readings the response convention is even subtler, except for laughter, but there are audible responses which the reader counts on just as the actor does.

I learned that once for all at a reading I did in Santa

Barbara. They had no lights on the audience, so I was facing this black chasm, and no sound came out of it. Total silence. Reading to pillows. Despair. Afterwards the students came around all warm and affectionate and said they'd loved it, but it was too late, I was a wreck. They'd been so laid back or so respectful or something they hadn't given me any response, and so they hadn't been working with me; and you can't do it alone.

It was men who first got poetry off the page, but the act was of great importance to women. Women have a particular stake in keeping the oral functions of literature alive, since misogyny wants women to be silent, and misogynist critics and academics do not want to hear the woman's voice in literature, in any sense of the word. There is solid evidence for the fact that when women speak more than thirty per cent of the time, men perceive them as dominating the conversation; well, similarly, if, say, two women in a row get one of the big annual literary awards, masculine voices start talking about feminist cabals, political correctness, and the decline of fairness in judging. The thirty per cent rule is really powerful. If more than one woman out of four or five won the Pulitzer, the PEN/ Faulkner, the Booker – if more than one woman in ten were to win the Nobel literature prize – the ensuing masculine furore would devalue and might destroy the prize. Apparently, literary guys can only compete with each other. Put on a genuinely equal competitive footing with women, they get hysterical. They just have to have their voices heard seventy per cent of the time.

Well, when feminism got reborn, it urged literary women to raise their voices, to yell unladylikely, to shoot for parity. So ever since, we have been grabbing the mike and letting loose. And it was this spirit of *hey, let's make a lot of noise* that carried me into experimenting with performance poetry.

124

Not performance art, where you take your clothes off and
dip yourself in chocolate or anything exciting like that,
I'm way too old for that to work at all well and also I am
a coward. But just letting my own voice loose, getting it
off the page. Making female noises, shrieking and squeaking and being shrill, all those things that annoy people
with longer vocal cords. Another case where the length of
organs seems to be so important to men.

I read this piece, 'Loud Cows', on tape at first but then
didn't know what to do with the tape, so I do it live; and
it's never twice the same, and though it has been printed, it
really needs you, the audience, to be there, going *eeso, eeso*!
So I'll end up now by performing it, in the hope of sending you away from this great conference with the memory
of seeing an old woman mooing loudly in public.

LOUD COWS

It's allowed. It is allowed, we are allowedSILENCE!
It is allowed. It IS allowed. It IS allowedSILENCE!!
it used to be allowed.
SI – EE – LENTSSSSS.
I-EE AM THE AWE –THOR.
REEEED MEEE IN SI-EE-LENT AWE.

but it's aloud.
it is aloud.

A word is a noise a word is a noise
A word is a NOISE a NOISE a NOISE –

AWWWWW.

The word is aloud. The word is a loud thing.
The loud word is allowed, aloud to be, the loud word
allows to be, it allows as how.

but
GUNS have si-len-cers.
Gumments have sssi-len-sssers.

So do Private SseC-tors.
Words are to be-hayve.
To lie sigh-lent-ly on pages being good.

To keep their covers over them.
Words are to be clean.
To be neat.
To be seen   not   heard.

Words are the children of the fathers who saySILENCE!
who say BANG! you're dead!

But:
the word is longer than daddy and louder than bang.
And all that silent words forbid DO NOT TRESPASS KEEP
                                        OUT SILENCE!
And all that silent words forbid, loud words allow to be.

All, all walls fall.

I say aloud: All walls all fall.
        It is aloud, it is allowed to be loud,
        and I say it is aloud LOUDly
        loudness allowing us to BE us – SO –

MOOOOOOOOOOOOOO**VE OH**-ver –

here come the LOUD COWS right NOW!

Mooooooooving throooooooough the silences

Mooooooooing in the Libraries

LOUD COWS in the sacred groves (*sssssh! don't wake daddy!*)

126

MOOO-OOOO-OOOOVE along there,

MOOOOOOVe along,
                    JUMP! over the
                              moooOOOOOOOON!

LOUD cows LOUD COWS
Loud SOWS LOUD SOWS now
        mouthing sounds**HEY!**
IT IS ALOUD!

THE SOUND OF YOUR WRITING (1998)

She slipped swift as a silvery fish
through the slapping gurgle of sea-waves.

The sound of the language is where it all begins. The test of a sentence is, Does it sound right? The basic elements of language are physical: the noise words make, the sounds and silences that make the rhythms marking their relationships. Both the meaning and the beauty of the writing depend on these sounds and rhythms. This is just as true of prose as it is of poetry, though the sound effects of prose are usually subtle and always irregular.

Most children enjoy the sound of language for its own sake. They wallow in repetitions and luscious word-sounds and the crunch and slither of onomatopoeia; they fall in love with musical or impressive words and use them in all the wrong places. Some writers keep this primal interest in and love for the sounds of language. Others 'outgrow' their oral/aural sense of what they're reading or writing. That's a dead loss. An awareness of what your own writing sounds like is an essential skill for a writer. Fortunately it's quite easy to cultivate, to learn or reawaken.

A good writer, like a good reader, has a mind's ear. We

mostly read prose in silence, but many readers have a keen inner ear that hears it. Dull, choppy, droning, jerky, feeble: these common criticisms of narrative are all faults in the sound of it. Lively, well-paced, flowing, strong, beautiful: these are all qualities of the sound of prose, and we rejoice in them as we read. Narrative writers need to train their mind's ear to listen to their own prose, to hear as they write.

The chief duty of a narrative sentence is to lead to the next sentence – to keep the story going. Forward movement, pace, and rhythm are words that are going to return often in this book. Pace and movement depend above all on rhythm, and the primary way you feel and control the rhythm of your prose is by hearing it – by listening to it.

Getting an act or an idea across isn't all a story does. A story is made out of language, and language can and does express delight in itself just as music does. Poetry isn't the only kind of writing that can sound gorgeous. Consider what's going on in these four examples. (Read them aloud! Read them aloud loudly!)

EXAMPLE I

The *Just So Stories* are a masterpiece of exuberant vocabulary, musical rhythms, and dramatic phrasing. Rudyard Kipling has let generations of kids know how nonsensically beautiful a story can sound. And there's nothing in either nonsense or beauty that restricts it to children.

Rudyard Kipling: from 'How the Rhinoceros Got His Skin' in *Just So Stories*

Once upon a time, on an uninhabited island on the shores of the Red Sea, there lived a Parsee from whose hat the rays of

130

the sun were reflected in more-than-oriental splendour. And
the Parsee lived by the Red Sea with nothing but his hat and
his knife and a cooking-stove of the kind that you must particularly never touch. And one day he took flour and water and
currants and plums and sugar and things, and made himself
one cake which was two feet across and three feet thick. It was
indeed a Superior Comestible (that's magic), and he put it on
the stove because he was allowed to cook on that stove, and he
baked it and he baked it till it was all done brown and smelt
most sentimental. But just as he was going to eat it there came
down to the beach from the Altogether Uninhabited Interior
one Rhinoceros with a horn on his nose, two piggy eyes, and
few manners. . . . And the Rhinoceros upset the oil-stove with
his nose, and the cake rolled on the sand, and he spiked that
cake on the horn of his nose, and he ate it, and he went away,
waving his tail, to the desolate and Exclusively Uninhabited
Interior which abuts on the islands of Mazanderan, Socotra,
and the Promontories of the Larger Equinox.

This passage from Mark Twain's early story 'The Celebrated
Jumping Frog of Calaveras County' is totally aural/oral, its
beauty lying in its irresistible dialectical cadences. There
are lots of ways to be gorgeous.

EXAMPLE II

Mark Twain: from 'The Celebrated Jumping Frog of
Calaveras County'

Well, thish-yer Smiley had rat-tarriers, and chicken cocks, and
tom cats and all them kind of things, till you couldn't rest,
and you couldn't fetch nothing for him to bet on but he'd
match you. He ketched a frog one day, and took him home,
and said he cal'lated to educate him; and so he never done

131

nothing for three months but set in his back yard and learn that frog to jump. And you bet you he did learn him, too. He'd give him a little punch behind, and the next minute you'd see that frog whirling in the air like a doughnut – see him turn one summerset, or maybe a couple, if he got a good start, and come down flat-footed and all right, like a cat. He got him up so in the matter of ketching flies, and kep' him in practice so constant, that he'd nail a fly every time as fur as he could see him. Smiley said all a frog wanted was education, and he could do 'most anything – and I believe him. Why, I've seen him set Dan'l Webster down here on this floor – Dan'l Webster was the name of the frog – and sing out, "Flies, Dan'l, flies!" and quicker'n you could wink he'd spring straight up and snake a fly off'n the counter there, and flop down on the floor ag'in as solid as a gob of mud, and fall to scratching the side of his head with his hind foot as indifferent as if he hadn't no idea he'd been doin' any more'n any frog might do. You never see a frog so modest and straightfor'ard as he was, for all he was so gifted. And when it come to fair and square jumping on a dead level, he could get over more ground at one straddle than any animal of his breed you ever see. Jumping on a dead level was his strong suit, you understand; and when it come to that, Smiley would ante up money on him as long as he had a red. Smiley was monstrous proud of his frog, and well he might be, for fellers that had traveled and been everywheres all said he laid over any frog that ever they see.

In the first example the more-than-oriental splendour of the language and in the second the irresistibly drawling aural cadences keep moving the story forward. In this one and the next, the vocabulary is simple and familiar; it's above all the rhythm that is powerful and effective. To read Hurston's sentences aloud is to be caught up in their music and beat, their hypnotic, fatal, forward drive.

EXAMPLE III

Zora Neale Hurston: from *Their Eyes Were Watching God*

So the beginning of this was a woman and she had come back from burying the dead. Not the dead of sick and ailing with friends at the pillow and the feet. She had come back from the sodden and the bloated; the sudden dead, their eyes flung wide open in judgment.

The people all saw her come because it was sundown. The sun was gone, but he had left his footprints in the sky. It was the time for sitting on porches beside the road. It was the time to hear things and talk. These sitters had been tongueless, ear-less, eyeless conveniences all day long. Mules and other brutes had occupied their skins. But now, the sun and the bossman were gone, so the skins felt powerful and human. They be-came lords of sounds and lesser things. They passed nations through their mouths. They sat in judgment.

Seeing the woman as she was made them remember the envy they had stored up from other times. So they chewed up the back parts of their minds and swallowed with relish. They made burning statements with questions, and killing tools out of laughs. It was mass cruelty. A mood come alive. Words walking without masters; walking together like harmony in a song.

In the next passage, Tom, a middle-aged rancher, is coping with the early onslaught of the cancer he knows will kill him. Molly Gloss's prose is quiet and subtle; its power and beauty come from the perfect placement and timing of the words, the music of their sound, and the way the changing sentence rhythms embody and express the emotions of the characters.

EXAMPLE IV

Molly Gloss: from *The Hearts of Horses*

His flock of chickens had already gone in roost, and the yard was quiet – chickens will begin to announce themselves hours before sunrise as if they can't wait for the day to get started but they are equally interested in an early bedtime. Tom had grown used to sleeping through their early-morning summons, all his family had, but in the last few weeks he'd been waking as soon as he heard the first hens peep, before even the roosters took up their reveille. The sounds they made in those first dark moments of the day had begun to seem to him as soft and devotional as an Angelus bell. And he had begun to dread the evenings – to wish, like the chickens, to climb into bed and close his eyes as soon as shadows lengthened and light began to seep out of the sky.

He let himself into the woodshed and sat down on a pile of stacked wood and rested his elbows on his knees and rocked himself back and forth. His body felt swollen with something inexpressible, and he thought if he could just weep he'd begin to feel better. He sat and rocked and eventually began to cry, which relieved nothing, but then he began to be racked with great coughing sobs that went on until whatever it was that had built up inside him had been slightly released. When his breathing eased, he went on sitting there rocking back and forth quite a while, looking at his boots, which were caked with manure and bits of hay. Then he wiped his eyes with his handkerchief and went into the house and sat down to dinner with his wife and son.

FURTHER READING

Alice Walker's *The Color Purple* is notable for the splendid sound of its language. For quietly powerful rhythms, look at Sarah Orne Jewett's *The Country of the Pointed Firs* or Kent Haruf's fine Western novel *Plainsong*.

Fantasy is a form of narrative essentially dependent on its language, and several classics of English prose, such as *Alice in Wonderland*, are fantasies. But keep your ear out when reading writers you mightn't associate with aural beauty; you may realise that much of the meaning has come to you through the sound and rhythm of the words.

EXERCISE ONE: BEING GORGEOUS

Part One

Write a paragraph to a page of narrative that's meant to be read aloud. Use onomatopoeia, alliteration, repetition, rhythmic effects, made-up words or names, dialect – any kind of sound effect you like – but NOT rhyme or metre.

I want you to write for pleasure – to play. Just listen to the sounds and rhythms of the sentences you write and play with them, like a kid with a kazoo. This isn't 'free writing', but it's similar in that you're relaxing control: you're encouraging the words themselves – the sounds of them, the beats and echoes – to lead you on. For the moment, forget all the good advice that says good style is invisible, good art conceals art. Show off! Use the whole orchestra our wonderful language offers us!

Write it for children, if that's the way you can give yourself permission to do it. Write it for your ancestors. Use any narrating voice you like. If you're familiar with a dialect or accent, use it instead of vanilla English. Be very noisy, or be hushed. Try to reproduce the action in the jerky or flowing movement of the words. Make what happens happen in the sounds of the words, the rhythms of the sentences. Have fun, cut loose, play around, repeat, invent, feel free.

Remember – no rhyme, no regular metre. This is prose, not poetry!

I hesitate to suggest any 'plot', but if you need some kind of hook to hang the language on, you might try telling the climax of a ghost story. Or invent an island and start walking across it – what happens?

Part Two
In a paragraph or so, describe an action, or a person feeling strong emotion – joy, fear, grief. Try to make the rhythm and movement of the sentences embody or represent the physical reality you're writing about.

Performing and listening to these pieces in a group can be a lot of fun. Not much critiquing will be called for. The best response to a successful performance piece is applause.

If you're working alone, read your pieces aloud; perform them with vigour. Doing so will almost certainly lead you to improve the text here and there, to play some more with it, to make the sound of it still stronger and livelier.

To think or talk about afterward: Did concentrating on the sound of the writing release or enable anything unusual or surprising, a voice you haven't often used? Did you enjoy being gorgeous, or was it a strain? Can you say why?

The question of self-consciously 'beautiful writing' is worthy of thought and discussion. How do you respond to the work of a novelist or essayist who visibly strives to write striking or poetical prose, using unusual or archaic words, combining words in a surprising way, going in for sound effects? Do you enjoy it? Does the conscious style do its work as prose? Does it intensify what it's saying or distract you from it?

Names are interesting sounds, and names of characters, the sound of them, the echo-allusions hidden in them, can be intensely expressive: Uriah Heep . . . Jane Eyre . . . Beloved . . . Names of places, too: Faulkner's Yoknapatawpha County, Tolkien's haunting Lothlórien or his simple yet deeply evocative Middle-earth. It can be fun to think about names in fiction and what it is about the sound of them that makes them meaningful.

Being Gorgeous is a highly repeatable exercise, by the way, and can serve as a warm-up to writing. Try to set a mood by using verbal sound effects. Look at the view out the window or the mess on the desk, or remember something that happened yesterday or something weird that somebody said, and make a gorgeous sentence or two or three out of it. It might get you into the swing.

AWARD AND GENDER
(1999)

Given as a talk and a handout at the Seattle Book Fair in 1999.

In 1998 I was on a jury of three choosing a literary prize. From 104 novels, we selected a winner and four books for the shortlist, arriving at consensus with unusual ease and unanimity. We were three women, and the books we chose were all written by women. The eldest and wisest of us said, Ouch! If a jury of women picks only women finalists, people will call us a feminist cabal and dismiss our choices as prejudiced, and the winning book will suffer for it.

I said, But if we were men and picked all books by men, nobody would say a damn thing about it.

True, said our Wise Woman, but we want our winner to have credibility, and the only way three women can have credibility as a jury is to have some men on the shortlist.

Against my heart and will, I agreed. And so two women who should have been there got bumped from our shortlist, and the two men whose books we had placed sixth and seventh got on it.

Literary awards used to be essentially literary events. Though a prize such as the Pulitzer certainly influenced the sale of the book, that wasn't all it was valued for. Since the takeover of most publishing houses by their accounting departments, the financial aspect of the literary award has become more and more important.

These days, literary prizes carry a huge weight in fame, money and shelf longevity.

But only some of them. Certain awards are newsworthy and success-assuring: most of them are not. The selection of which prize is sure to hit the headlines and which is ignored seems to be almost totally arbitrary. The media follow habit without question. Hysteria about the Booker Prize is assured; general indifference to the PEN Western States Award is certain.

Most writers who have served on award juries agree that the field of finalists is often so qualitatively even that selection of a single winner is essentially arbitrary. Many also agree that the field of finalists often contains books so various in nature and intent that the selection of a single winner is, again, essentially arbitrary. But a single winner is what is demanded of them, so they provide it. Then publishers capitalise on it, bookstores fawn on it, libraries stock their shelves with it, while the shortlist books are forgotten.

I feel that the competitive, single-winner pattern is suited to sports events but not to literature, that the increasingly exaggerated dominance of the 'big' awards in the field of fiction is pernicious, and that the system inevitably perpetuates cronyism, geographical favouritism, gender favouritism and big-name syndrome.

Of these, gender favouritism particularly irks me. It is so often and so indignantly denied that I began to wonder if I was irked over nothing. I decided to try to find if my impression that the great majority of literary awards went to men had any foundation in fact. To establish my facts, I limited my study to fiction.

If more men than women publish fiction, that would of course justify an imbalance towards male prizewinners. So to start with I did some gender sampling of authors of novels and story collections published in various periods from 1996 to 1998. My time was limited and my method was crude. The numbers (only about a thousand writers in all) may not be large enough to be statistically significant. My author-gender count covers only four recent years, while my figures on the awards go back decades. (A study on author gender in fiction in the whole twentieth century would be a very interesting subject for a thesis.) My sources were *Publishers Weekly* for general fiction, *What Do I Read Next?* for genre fiction, and the *Hornbook* for children's books. I counted authors by sex, omitting collaborations and any names that were not gender identifiable. (My genre sources identified aliases. Rumour has it that many romances are written by men under female pen names, but I found only one transgenderer* – a woman mystery writer who used a male name.)

---

* Editors' note: Le Guin appears to be coining this noun to refer to a choice by a writer to use a pen name not of their gender assigned at birth, without implying that the writer is or is not trans, or with any negative expression towards trans writers. Le Guin may have been particularly aware of the question of AFAB writers using male names, whatever their gender identity, due to her long friendship with James Tiptree Jr, whose revelation that their birth name was Alice Sheldon caused Le Guin to re-evaluate how she had read her admired friend's work for over a decade, and indeed to re-evaluate her ideas on gendered writing.

Author Gender

Summations
(see Details of the Counts and Awards, below)

> General fiction: 192 men, 167 women: slightly more men than women.
> Genre fiction: 208 men, 250 women: more women than men.
> Children's books and young adult: 83 men, 161 women: twice as many women as men.
> All genres: 483 men, 578 women: about 5 women to 4 men.

Eighty of the authors in my Genre category were romance writers, all women; if you consider them as probably balanced by predominantly male-written genres such as sports, war and porn, which I did not have figures for, you might arrive at parity. It looks as if, overall, as many women as men, perhaps slightly more women than men, write and publish novels and stories.

Author gender in fiction is pretty near 1:1.

Now for the gender counts and ratios for literary prizes. Ideally I would have listed the shortlists or runners-up where available, but given the shortness of time in which I had to prepare this paper, and the shortness of life, I list only winners. (Information on most awards, including shortlists, winners and sometimes jurors, is accessible at libraries and on the Net.)

The years covered are the years the prize has been given, up to 1998 – these spans of course vary greatly. The oldest is the Nobel Prize in Literature.

I did not try to find out the gender composition of the juries of any of these awards, though many are on record.

I wish I had the time to go into this and find out whether juries are gender balanced or not, whether the balance has changed over time, and whether gender composition influences their choices. One might well assume that men tend to pick men and women women, but if juries are even moderately balanced between men and women, my figures do not support this assumption. It looks as if men and women tend to pick men.

Most awards are chosen by a judge or panel of judges, but some genre prizes are voted by readers or (in the case of the Nebula Award) fellow writers in the genre.

(In this context I want to point out that the MacArthur 'genius awards' are nominated by 'experts' chosen by the MacArthur Foundation, and the winners are selected by a board chosen by the Foundation – a permanently secret board, whose members are therefore, in the true meaning of the word, irresponsible. In all the arts awards given by the MacArthur Foundation, I find the 3:1 gender ratio – three men to one woman – so consistent that I must assume it is the result of deliberate policy.)

Gender Ratio of Literary Prizes, Male to Female
(in order of most extreme imparity to nearest parity)

Nobel Prize in Literature, 10:1
PEN/Faulkner Award for Fiction, 8:1
Edgar Grand Master Award (mystery), 7:1
National Book Award (now American Book Award), 6:1
World Fantasy Lifetime Achievement Award, 6:1
Pulitzer Prize for Literature, since 1943, 5:1
Edgar Award for Best Novel, since 1970 (mystery), 5:1
Hugo Award (science fiction) (reader vote), 3:1
World Fantasy Best Novel Award, 3:1
Newbery Award (juvenile), 3:1

Nebula Award (science fiction) (voted by fellow writers), 2.4:1

Pulitzer Prize for Literature, till 1943, 2:1

Edgar Award for Best Novel, till 1970 (mystery), 2:1

Booker Prize, 2:1

Some Observations

Though the number of men and women writing literary fiction is nearly equal, the 'big' literary awards, Nobel, National Book Award, Booker, PEN, Pulitzer, give 5.5 prizes to men for every 1 to a woman. Genre awards average 4 to 1, so a woman stands a better chance of getting a prize if she writes genre fiction.

Among all the prizes I counted, the ratio is 4.5:1 – for every woman who gets a fiction prize, four and a half men do; or, to avoid the uncomfortable idea of half-men, you can say that nine men get a prize for every two women who do.

Except in the Nobel, which gave three women prizes in the nineties, there was no gain in gender parity in these prizes during the twentieth century, and in some cases a drastic decline. I broke the figures for the Pulitzer into before and after 1943, and the Edgar Best Novel into before and after 1970, to demonstrate the most notable examples of this decline. There would have to have been a massive change in author gender, a great increase in the number of men writing fiction in these fields, to explain or justify the increasing percentage of male award winners. I do not have the figures, but my impression is that there has not been any such great increase; my guess is that the fifty-fifty ratio of men and women writing fiction has been fairly constant through the twentieth century.

In children's literature, where by my rough count there

are twice as many women authors, men win three times as many prizes as women.

Nearly two-thirds of mystery writers are women, but men get three times as many prizes as women, and since 1970, five times as many.

The inescapable conclusion is that prize juries, whether they consist of readers, writers or pundits, through conscious or unconscious prejudice, reward men four and a half times more than women.

The escapable conclusion is that men write fiction four and a half times better than women. This conclusion appears to be acceptable to many people, so long as it goes unspoken.

Those of us who do not find it acceptable have to speak.

Literary juries and the sponsors of awards need to have their prejudices queried and their consciousness raised. The perpetuation of gender prejudice through literary prizes should be challenged by fairminded writers by discussions such as this, by further and better research, and by letters of comment and protest to the awarding bodies, to literary publications, and to the press.

Details of the Counts and Awards

This appendix is for people who enjoy details and want to see how my system of determining author gender and gender parity worked, or suggest how it might be improved, enlarged and updated – a job I would gladly hand on to anybody who wants to undertake it . . . And I have made some notes and observations on various outcomes and oddities.

AUTHOR GENDER (NOVELS AND STORY COLLECTIONS)
(MF indicates male to female)

'Literary' Fiction
Hardcover: men 128, women 98. MF ratio 1.3:1
Trade paperback: men 64, women 69. MF ratio near
    parity

'Genre' Fiction
Mystery: men 52, women 72. MF ratio 0.7:1
Romance: men 0, women 80. MF ratio 0:1
Western: men 60, women 22. MF ration 3:1
Fantasy: men 39, women 40. MF ratio near parity.
Science fiction: men 57, women 35. MF ratio 1.6:1

'Juvenile' Fiction
Children, age 6-12: men 80, women 117. MF ratio
    0.7:1
Young adult: men 23, women 44. MF ratio 1:2

SUMMARY

'Literary' fiction: men 192, women 167
'Genre' fiction: men 208, women 249
'Juvenile' fiction: men 103, women 161

These categories, derived from my reference sources,
should be taken with extreme distrust, which is why I put
them in quotes. Genre, as generally understood, is itself a
suspect concept. Many of the books could well have been
listed in two or even three categories.

Total authors: 1080
Men 503, women 577
Approximate MF ratio 5:6

AUTHOR GENDER IN AWARDS GIVEN TO NOVELS
AND STORY COLLECTIONS

The Nobel Prize in Literature (voted by a special board)

Between 1901 and 1998, the prize was given 91 times (it was not given 7 times, notably during World War Two). It has been split twice between two men and once between a man and a woman, so that the totals have decimals.

Men 85.5, women 8.5. MF ratio almost exactly 10:1

The years women were given the Nobel for Literature were 1909, 1926, 1928, 1938, 1945, 1966, 1991, 1993, 1996: pretty much one woman per decade, till the nineties when three women were given prizes.

THE PULITZER PRIZE FOR LITERATURE
(VOTED BY A JURY OF WRITERS)

Given since 1918, with six no-award years.

Men 50, women 23. MF ratio just over 2:1

The ratio has declined severely from parity since 1943. Of the 23 awards to women, 12 were given in the 25 years 1918-1943, but only 11 in the 54 years 1944-1998. Since 1943, though half or more of the shortlist authors are often women, 5 out of 6 winners have been men (MF ratio 5:1).

THE BOOKER PRIZE
(VOTED BY A JURY OF WRITERS AND CRITICS)

Given since 1969.

Men 21, women 11. MF ratio 2:1

This ratio has been pretty steady over 30 years, remaining the nearest parity of the prizes I examined.

THE NATIONAL BOOK AWARD/AMERICAN BOOK AWARD

Given since 1950, with various types of jury, various sponsors, and several changes of category in fiction, so it is hard to count. As well as I can determine, the 'Best Novel' award (excluding genre and juvenile) has been as follows:

Men 43, women 7. MF ratio 6:1

THE PEN/FAULKNER AWARD FOR FICTION (VOTED BY A JURY)

Given since 1981.

Men 17, women 2. MF ratio 8.5: 1

As there are always women on the shortlist for the PEN/Faulkner, I was startled, in fact shocked, to discover how few have been given the award. This prize is almost as male oriented as the Nobel.

THE NEBULA AWARD (SCIENCE FICTION AND FANTASY; VOTED BY PUBLIC NOMINATION AND SECRET BALLOT OF MEMBERS OF THE SCIENCE FICTION AND FANTASY WRITERS' ASSOCIATION)

Given since 1965.

Men 24, women 10. MF ratio 2.4:1

Given since 1953.

   Men 36, women 11. MF ratio 3:1

I find it interesting that these two balloted awards, the
Nebula selected by writers and the Hugo by fans, are nearer parity than several juried awards, and far nearer parity
than the similarly balloted Edgar.

THE WORLD FANTASY AWARD
(GIVEN BY A JURY, PLUS AN ANONYMOUS DECISION)

Best Novel (split awards cause decimals):

   Men 18.5, women 5.5. MF ratio 3:1

Lifetime Achievement (16 awards plus a 5-way split):

   Men 17, women 3. MF ratio 6:1

THE EDGAR AWARD

Best Novel (mystery; voted by the members of the Mystery
Writers of America)

Given since 1946.

   Men 39, women 13. MF ratio 3:1

This ratio is for the whole 52 years. From 1946 to 1970,
16 men and 8 women were given the prize, making the
ratio 2:1. But in the 28 years since 1970, despite the fact
that considerably more women than men write mysteries,
only 5 women have won 'Best Novel,' making the MF
ratio almost 5:1.

GRAND MASTER

First given in 1955, to Agatha Christie. For the next 15 years, only men were made Grand Masters. By 1998, of the 46 Grand Masters, 35 were men, 8 women – but 3 of those 8 women shared a single award. No men have been asked to share their Grand Mastery. Counting the 3-in-1 as a single award, the MF ratio is 7:1.

THE NEWBERY AWARD (FOR EXCELLENCE IN CHILDREN'S LITERATURE; VOTED BY A 'PANEL OF EXPERTS')

Given since 1922.

1922-1930, all the awards went to men; 1931-1940, all to women. From 1941-1998, men 16, women 40. As about 1 out of 3 authors of books for children and young adults is a man, the prize is a pretty fair reflection of author gender.

ON GENETIC DETERMINISM
(2003)

I wrote this piece as a reader's personal response to a text. Finding myself troubled by many of E.O.Wilson's sweeping statements, I tried to figure out what was troubling me. I did it in writing because I think best in writing. An amateur responding to a professional is likely to make a fool of herself, and no doubt I've done just that; but I decided to publish the piece. I am not pitting my opinions against scientific observation; I am pitting my opinions against a scientist's opinions. Opinions and assumptions, when presented by a distinguished scientist, are likely to be mistaken for scientific observations — for fact. And that was what troubled me.

In his very interesting autobiography, *Naturalist*, E.O. Wilson summarises the statement of the biological foundations of human behaviour made in his book *Sociobiology*:

> Genetic determinism, the central objection raised against [Sociobiology], is the bugbear of the social sciences. So what I said that can indeed be called genetic determinism needs saying here again. My argument ran essentially as follows: Human beings inherit a propensity to acquire behavior and social structures, a propensity that is shared by enough people to be called human nature. The defining traits include division

of labor between the sexes, bonding between parents and children, heightened altruism toward closest kin, incest avoidance, other forms of ethical behavior, suspicion of strangers, tribalism, dominance orders within groups, male dominance overall, and territorial aggression over limiting [limited?] resources. Although people have free will and the choice to turn in many directions, the channels of their psychological development are nevertheless – however much we might wish otherwise – cut more deeply by the genes in certain directions than in others. So while cultures vary greatly, they inevitably converge toward these traits . . . The important point is that heredity interacts with environment to create a gravitational pull toward a fixed mean. It gathers people in all societies into the narrow statistical circle that we define as human nature.

That human beings inherit a propensity to acquire behaviour and that the construction of society is one of these behaviours, I agree. Whether anything worth the risk is to be gained by calling this propensity 'human nature', I wonder. Anthropologists have excellent justification for avoiding the term human nature, for which no agreed definition exists, and which all too easily, even when intended as descriptive, is applied prescriptively.

Wilson states that the traits he lists constitute a 'narrow statistical circle that we define as human nature'. Like Tonto, I want to ask, 'Who "we", white man?' The selection of traits is neither complete nor universal, the definitions seem sloppy rather than narrow, and the statistics are left to the imagination. More statistics and completer definitions are to be found in *Sociobiology*, of course; but Wilson's own statement of what the book says is as accurate and complete as it is succinct, so that I think it fair to address my arguments to it.

Taking it, then, phrase by phrase:

Division of labour between the sexes:
This phrase means only that in all or most known societies men and women do different kinds of work; but since it is very seldom understood in that strict meaning, it is either ingenuous or disingenuous to use it in this context without acknowledging its usual implications. Unless those implications are specifically denied, the phrase 'division of labour between the sexes' is understood by most readers in this society to imply specific kinds of gender-divided work, and so to imply that these are genetically determined: our genes ensure that men hunt, women gather; men fight, women nurse; men go forth, women keep the house; men do art, women do domestic work; men function in the 'public sphere', women in the 'private', and so on.

No anthropologist or person with an anthropological conscience, knowing how differently work is gendered in different societies, could accept these implications. I don't know what implications, if any, Wilson intended. But as this kind of unstated extension of reductionist statements does real intellectual and social damage, reinforcing prejudices and bolstering bigotries, it behoves a responsible scientist to define his terms more carefully.

As some gendered division of labour exists in every society, I would fully agree with Wilson if he had used a more careful phrasing, such as 'some form of gender construction, including gender-specific activities'.

Bonding between parents and children; heightened altruism toward closest kin; suspicion of strangers:
All these behaviours are related, and can be defined as forms of 'selfish gene' behaviour; I think they have been shown to be as nearly universal among human beings as

153

among other social animals. But in human beings such behaviour is uniquely, and universally, expressed in so immense a range of behaviours and social structures, of such immense variety and complexity, that one must ask if this range and complexity, not present in any animal behaviour, is not as genetically determined as the tendencies themselves.

If my question is legitimate, then Wilson's statement is unacceptably reductive. To focus on a type of human behaviour shared with other animals, but to omit from the field of vision the unique and universal character of such behaviour among humans, is to beg the question of how far genetic determination of behaviour may extend. Yet that is a question that no sociobiologist can beg.

Tribalism:

I understand tribalism to mean an extension of the behaviour just mentioned: social groups are extended beyond immediate blood kin by identifying nonkin as 'socially kin' and strangers as nonstrangers, establishing shared membership in constructs such as clan, moiety, language group, race, nation, religion and so on.

I can't imagine what the mechanism would be that made this kind of behaviour genetically advantageous, but I think it is as universal among human groups as the behaviours based on actual kinship. If universality of a human behaviour pattern means that it is genetically determined, then this type of behaviour must have a genetic justification. I think it would be a rather hard one to establish, but I'd like to see a sociobiologist try.

Incest avoidance:

Here I'm uncertain about the evolutionary mechanism that enables the selfish gene to recognise a selfish gene that is too closely akin, and so determines a behaviour norm. If there are social mechanisms preventing incest among the other primates, I don't know them. (Driving young males out of the alpha male's group is male-dominant behaviour serving only incidentally and ineffectively as incest prevention; the alpha male does mate with his sisters and daughters, though the young males have to go find somebody else's.)

I'd like to know whether Wilson knows what the general incidence of incest among mammals is, and whether he believes that incest is 'avoided' among humans any more than it is among apes, cats, wild horses and so on. Do all human societies ban incest? I don't know; it was an open question, last I heard. That most human societies have cultural strictures against certain types of incest is true; that many human societies fail as often as not to implement them is also true. I think in this case Wilson has confused a common cultural dictum or desideratum with actual behaviour; or else he is saying that our genes programme us to *say* we must not do something, but do not prevent us from *doing* it. Now those are some fancy genes.

Dominance orders within groups:
Here I suspect Wilson's anthropology is influenced by behaviourists' experiments with chickens and primatologists' observations of apes more than by anthropologists' observation of human behaviour in groups. Dominance order is very common in human societies, but so are other forms of group relationship, such as maintaining order through consensus; there are whole societies in which dominance is not the primary order, and groups in most societies in which dominance does not function at all, difficult as this may be to believe at Harvard. Wilson's statement is suspect in emphasising one aspect of behaviour

while omitting others. Once again, it is reductive. It would be more useful if phrased more neutrally and more accurately: perhaps, 'tendency to establish structured or fluid social relationships outside immediate kinship'.

Male dominance overall:
This is indeed the human social norm. I take it that the genetic benefit is that which is supposed to accrue in all species in which the male displays to the female to attract her choice and/or drives away weaker males from his mate or harem, thus ensuring that his genes will dominate in the offspring (the *male* selfish gene). Species in which this kind of behaviour does not occur (including so close a genetic relative as the bonobo) are apparently not considered useful comparisons or paradigms for human behaviour.

That male aggressivity and display behaviour extend from sexuality to all forms of human social and cultural activity is indubitable. Whether this extension has been an advantage or a liability to our genetic survival is certainly arguable, probably unprovable. It certainly cannot simply be assumed to be of genetic advantage in the long run to the human, or even the male human, gene. The 'interaction of heredity with environment' in this case has just begun to be tested, since only in the last hundred years has there been a possibility of *unlimited* dominance by any subset of humanity, along with *unlimited*, uncontrollable aggressivity.

Territorial aggression over limiting [sic] resources:
This is evidently a subset of 'male dominance overall'. As I understand it, women's role in territorial aggression has been subsidiary, not institutionalised, and seldom even recognised socially or culturally. So far as I know, all organised and socially or culturally sanctioned aggression over

resources or at territorial boundaries is entirely controlled and almost wholly conducted by men.

It is flagrantly false to ascribe such aggression to scarcity of resources. Most wars in the historical period have been fought over quite imaginary, arbitrary boundaries. It is my impression of warlike cultures such as the Sioux or the Yanomamo that male aggression has no economic rationale at all. The phrase should be cut to 'territorial aggression', and attached to the 'male dominance' item.

Other forms of ethical behaviour:
This one's the big weasel. What forms of ethical behaviour? Ethical according to whose ethics?
Without invoking the dreaded bogey of cultural relativism, I think we have a right to ask anybody who asserts that there are universal human moralities to list and define them. If he asserts that they are genetically determined, he should be able to specify the genetic mechanism and the evolutionary advantage they involve.

Wilson appends these 'other forms' to 'incest avoidance', which is thus syntactically defined as ethical behaviour. Incest avoidance certainly involves some genetic advantage. If there are other behaviours that involve genetic advantage and are universally recognised as ethical, I want to know what they are.

Not beating up old ladies might be one. Grandmothers have been proved to play a crucial part in the survival of grandchildren in circumstances of famine and stress. Their genetic interest of course is clear. I doubt, however, that Wilson had grandmothers in mind.

Mother-child bonding might be one of his 'other forms of ethical behaviour.' It is tendentious, if not hypocritical, to call it 'bonding between parents and children' as Wilson does, since it is by no means a universal cultural

157

expectation that the male human parent will, or should, bond with his child. The biological father is replaced in many cultures by the mother's brother, or serves only as authority figure, or (as in our culture) is excused from responsibility for children he sired with women other than his current wife. A further danger in this context is that the mother-child bond is so often defined as 'natural' as to be interpreted as subethical. A mother who does not bond with her child is defined less as immoral than as inhuman. This is an example of why I think the whole matter of ethics, in this context, is a can of actively indefinable worms far better left unopened.

Perhaps that's why Wilson left these 'other ethical behaviours' so vague. Also, if he had specified as ethical such behaviour as, say, cooperation and mutual aid between individuals not blood kin, he would have risked his credibility with his fellow biologists still trained to interpret behaviour strictly in the mechanistic mode.

Finally, I wonder if genetic determinism as such really is 'the bugbear of the social sciences'. Academics are the very model of territorialism, and some social scientists certainly responded with fear and fury to what they saw as Wilson's aggression when he published *Sociobiology*. But on the whole, Wilson's statement seems a little paranoid, or a little boastful.

The controversy and animus aroused by Sociobiology might have been avoided if the author had presented his determinism in more precise, more careful, less tendentious, less anthropologically naive terms. If in fact his theory is not a bugbear to the social sciences, it's because it has not proved itself useful or even relevant to them.

I'd find his arguments far more interesting if he had genuinely taken pains to extend his reductive theory to explain specifically human behaviour, including the elaboration of the gender-based, kinbased repertory of behaviours we share with animals into the apparently infinite varieties of human social structures and the endless complexities of culture. But he has not done so.

There are social scientists and humanists, as well as determinists, who would argue that it's the vast range and complexity of human behavioural options, in origin genetically determined, that gives us what may ultimately be the illusion of free will. But Wilson, having raised this question in *Naturalist*, ducks right under it with a flat statement of belief that 'people have free will'. The statement as such is meaningless. I am not interested in his beliefs. He is not a religious thinker or a theologian but a scientist. He should speak as such.

OLD BODY NOT WRITING
(2003)

Some bits of this went into a piece called 'Writer's Block' for the New York Times Syndicate, *and a small part went into* Steering the Craft. *It is a rambling meditation that I came back to on and off over several years, when I wasn't writing what I wanted to be writing.*

Just now I'm not writing. That is, I'm writing here and now that I'm not writing, because I am unhappy about not writing. But if I have nothing to write I have nothing to write. Why can't I wait in patience till I do? Why is the waiting hard?

Because I am not as good at anything else and nothing else is as good. I would rather be writing than anything else.

Not because it is a direct pleasure in the physical sense, like a good dinner or sex or sunlight. Composition is hard work, involving the body not in satisfying activity and release but only in stillness and tension. It is usually accompanied by uncertainty as to the means and the outcome, and often surrounded by a kind of driving anxiety ('I have to finish this before I die and finishing it is going to kill me'). In any case, while actually composing, I'm in a kind of trance state that isn't pleasant or anything else. It has no qualities. It is unconsciousness of self. While writing I am unconscious of my existence or any existence except in the words as they sound and make rhythms and connect and make syntax and in the story as it happens.

Aha, then writing is an escape? (Oh the Puritan overtones in that word!) An escape from dissatisfactions, incompetences, woes? Yes, no doubt. And also a compensation for lack of control over life, for powerlessness. Writing, I'm in power, I control, I choose the words and shape the story. Don't I?

Do I? Who's I? Where's I while I write? Following the beat. The words. They're in control. It's the story that has the power. I'm what follows it, records it. That's my job, and the work is in doing my job right.

We use *escape* and *compensation* negatively, and so we can't use them to define the act of making, which is positive and irreducible to anything but itself. True making is truly satisfying. It is more truly satisfying than anything I know.

So when I have nothing to write I have nothing to escape to, nothing to compensate with, nothing to give control to, no power to share in, and no satisfaction. I have to just be here being old and worried and muddling and afraid that nothing makes sense. I miss and want that thread of words that runs through day and night leading me through the labyrinth of the years. I want a story to tell. What will give me one?

Having a clear time to write, often I sit and think hard, forcefully, powerfully, and make up interesting people and interesting situations from which a story could grow. I write them down, I work at them. But nothing grows. I am trying to make something happen, not waiting till it happens. I don't have a story. I don't have the person whose story it is.

When I was young, I used to know that I had a story to

write when I found in my mind and body an imaginary person whom I could embody myself in, with whom I could identify strongly, deeply, bodily. It was so much like falling in love that maybe that's what it was.

That's the physical side of storytelling, and it's still mysterious to me. Since I was in my sixties it has happened again (with Teyeo and Havzhiva in *Four Ways to Forgiveness*, for example) to my great delight, for it's an active, intense delight, to be able to live in the character night and day, have the character living in me, and their world overlapping and interplaying with my world. But I didn't embody so deeply with anybody in *Searoad*, nor with most of my characters in the last ten or fifteen years. Yet writing *Tehanu* or 'Sur' or 'Hernes' was as exciting as anything I ever did, and the satisfaction was solid.

I still find embodying or identifying most intense when the character is a man − when the body is absolutely not my own. That reach or leap across gender has an inherent excitement in it (which is probably why it is like falling in love). My identification with women characters such as Tenar or Virginia or Dragonfly is different. There is an even more sexual aspect to it, but not genital sexuality. Deeper. In the middle of my body, where you centre from in t'ai chi, where the chi is. That is where my women live in me.

This embodying business may be different for men and women (if other writers do it at all − how do I know?). But I incline to believe Virginia Woolf was right in thinking that the real thing goes on way past gender. Norman Mailer may seriously believe that you have to have balls to be a writer. If you want to write the way he writes I suppose you do. To me a writer's balls are irrelevant if not annoying. Balls aren't where the action is. When I say the middle of the body I don't mean balls, prick, cunt or womb. Sexualist reductionism is as bad as any other kind. If not worse.

When I had a hysterectomy, I worried about my writing, because sexualist reductionism had scared me. But I'm sure it wasn't as bad for me as losing his balls would be for a man like Norman Mailer. Never having identified my sex, my sexuality or my writing with my fertility, I didn't have to trash myself. I was able, with some pain and fear but not dreadful pain and fear, to think about what the loss meant to me as a writer, a person in a body who writes.

What it felt like to me was that in losing my womb I had indeed lost some connection, a kind of easy, bodily imagination, that had to be replaced, if it could be replaced, by the mental imagination alone. For a while I thought that I could not embody myself in an imagined person as I used to. I thought I couldn't 'be' anyone but me.

I don't mean that when I had a womb I believed that I carried characters around in it like foetuses. I mean that when I was young I had a complete, unthinking, bodily connection and emotional apprehension of my imagined people.

Now (perhaps because of the operation, perhaps through mere ageing) I was obliged to make the connection deliberately in the mind. I had to reach out with a passion that was not simply physical. I had to 'be' other people in a more radical, complete way.

This wasn't necessarily a loss. I began to see it might be a gain, forcing me to take the more risky way. The more intelligence the better, so long as the passion, the bodily emotional connection is made, is there.

Essays are in the head, they don't have bodies the way stories do: that's why essays can't satisfy me in the long run. But headwork is better than nothing, as witness me right now, making strings of words to follow through the maze of the day (a very simple maze: one or two choices, a food pellet for a reward). Any string of meaningfully connected words is better than none.

If I can find intensely felt meaning in the words or invest them with it, better yet – whether the meaning be intellectual, as now, or consist in their music, in which case I would, ¡ojalá! be writing poetry.

Best of all is if they find bodies and begin to tell a story.

Up there I said 'be' somebody, 'have the person', 'find the person'. This is the mystery.

I use the word *have* not in the sense of 'having' a baby, but in the sense of 'having' a body. To have a body is to be embodied. Embodiment is the key.

My plans for stories that don't become stories all lack that key, the person or people whose story it is, the heart, the soul, the embodied inwardness of a person or several people. When I am working on a story that isn't going to work, I make people up. I could describe them the way the how-to-write books say to do. I know their function in the story. I write about them – but I haven't found them, or they haven't found me. They don't inhabit me, I don't inhabit them. I don't have them. They are bodiless. So I don't have a story.

But as soon as I make this inward connection with a character, I know it body and soul, I have that person, I am that person. To have the person (and with the person, mysteriously, comes the name) is to have the story. Then I can begin writing directly, trusting the person knows where she or he is going, what will happen, what it's all about.

This is extremely risky, but it works for me, these days, more often than it used to. And it makes for a story that is without forced or extraneous elements, all of a piece, uncontrolled by intrusions of opinion, willpower, fear (of unpopularity, censorship, the editor, the market, whatever) or other irrelevancies.

So my search for a story, when I get impatient, is not so

much looking for a topic or subject or nexus or resonance or place-time (though all that is or will be involved) as casting about in my head for a stranger. I wander about the mental landscape looking for somebody, an Ancient Mariner or a Miss Bates, who will (almost certainly not when I want them, not when I invite them, not when I long for them, but at the most inconvenient and impossible time) begin telling me their story and not let me go until it's told.

The times when nobody is in the landscape are silent and lonely. They can go on and on until I think nobody will ever be there again but one stupid old woman who used to write books. But it's no use trying to populate it by willpower. These people come only when they're ready, and they do not answer to a call. They answer silence.

Many writers now call any period of silence a 'block'.

Would it not be better to look on it as a clearing? A way to go till you get where you need to be?

If I want to write and have nothing to write I do indeed feel blocked, or rather chocked – full of energy but nothing to spend it on, knowing my craft but nothing to use it on. It is frustrating, wearing, infuriating. But if I fill the silence with constant noise, writing anything in order to be writing something, forcing my willpower to invent situations for stories, I may be blocking myself. It's better to hold still and wait and listen to the silence. It's better to do some kind of work that keeps the body following a rhythm but doesn't fill up the mind with words.

I have called this waiting 'listening for a voice'. It has been that, a voice. It was that in 'Hernes', all through, when I'd wait and wait, and then the voice of one of the women would come and speak through me.

But it's more than voice. It's a bodily knowledge. Body is story; voice tells it.

WHAT IT WAS LIKE
(2004)

A talk given at a meeting of Oregon NARAL in January 2004.

My friends at NARAL asked me to tell you what it was like before *Roe vs. Wade*. They asked me to tell you what it was like to be twenty and pregnant in 1950 and when you tell your boyfriend you're pregnant, he tells you about a friend of his in the army whose girl told him she was pregnant, so he got all his buddies to come and say, 'We all fucked her, so who knows who the father is?' And he laughs at the good joke.

They asked me to tell you what it was like to be a pregnant girl – we weren't 'women' then – a pregnant college girl who, if her college found out she was pregnant, would expel her, there and then, without plea or recourse. What it was like, if you were planning to go to graduate school and get a degree and earn a living so you could support yourself and do the work you loved – what it was like to be a senior at Radcliffe and pregnant and if you bore this child, this child which the law demanded you bear and would then call 'unlawful', 'illegitimate', this child whose father denied it, this child which would take from you your capacity to support yourself and do the work you knew it was your gift and your responsibility to do: What

167

was it like?

I can hardly imagine what it's like to live as a woman under Fundamentalist Islamic law. I can hardly remember now, fifty-four years later, what it was like to live under Fundamentalist Christian law. Thanks to *Roe vs. Wade*, none of us in America has lived in that place for half a lifetime.

But I can tell you what it is like, for me, right now. It's like this: If I had dropped out of college, thrown away my education, depended on my parents through the pregnancy, birth, and infancy, till I could get some kind of work and gain some kind of independence for myself and the child, if I had done all that, which is what the anti-abortion people want me to have done, I would have borne a child for them, for the anti-abortion people, the authorities, the theorists, the fundamentalists; I would have borne a child for them, their child.

But I would not have borne my own first child, or second child, or third child. My children.

The life of that foetus would have prevented, would have aborted, three other foetuses, or children, or lives, or whatever you choose to call them: my children, the three I bore, the three wanted children, the three I had with my husband – whom, if I had not aborted the unwanted one, I would never have met and married, because he would have been a Fulbright student going to France on the *Queen Mary* in 1953 but I would not have been a Fulbright student going to France on the *Queen Mary* in 1953. I would have been an 'unwed mother' of a three-year-old in California, without work, with half an education, living off her parents, not marriageable, contributing nothing to her community but another mouth to feed, another useless woman.

But it is the children I have to come back to, my children Elisabeth, Caroline, Theodore, my joy, my pride, my loves. If I had not broken the law and aborted that life nobody

168

wanted, they would have been aborted by a cruel, bigoted, and senseless law. They would never have been born. This thought I cannot bear. I beg you to see what it is that we must save, and not to let the bigots and misogynists take it away from us again. Save what we won: our children. You who are young, before it's too late, save your children.

WHAT WOMEN KNOW
(2010)

Revised from two talks given at the Winter Fishtrap Gathering in Joseph, Oregon, in February 2010. Each talk preceded open group discussion of the topic.

THE FIRST EVENING

Our topic for tonight is: What do we learn from women?

Many of us find ourselves surprisingly defensive on the subject of how men's and women's roles differ, how gender is constructed and enacted. Since generalisations about human behaviour are easy to derail by bringing up exceptions, I suggest that to keep our discussion profitable, we footnote the exceptions. We're entering the Forest of Gender, where it's awfully easy to get lost. If we keep foregrounding a tree here and a tree there, we'll lose sight of the very big, dark woods we're trying to find a way through.

So, in answer to the question What do we learn from women? my first huge generalisation is that we learn how to be human.

Over the millennia, in all societies, right up to now in Oregon, women have supplied most of the basic instructions on how to walk, talk, eat, sing, pray, play with other children, and which adults we should respect, and what to fear, what to love – the basic skills, the basic rules. The whole amazing, complicated business of staying alive and being a member of a society.

In most times and most places, babies and little children have been taught predominantly, often solely, by mothers, grandmothers, aunts, neighbours, village women, pre-school and kindergarten teachers. And this continues in America now. Every time you see a young mother with her kids in the supermarket, you see a life-scholar, a teacher teaching an incredibly complex curriculum. Whether she does it well or not so well doesn't affect the rule: Most of the time, it's she who does it.

The basic skills she teaches are largely genderless. Boys and girls both learn them. As they become social skills, they may be coloured blue or pink, as when a girl is taught to be quiet and civil among adults while a boy is taught to yell and pester, or when a girl is praised for dancing with flowers on her head while a boy is shamed for it. But overall, the elemental skills and manners taught by women obtain for both genders.

By contrast, what young children learn from men is often gendered. Men may be more interested than women in making sure the pink and the blue don't mix. Fathers often teach their children sex roles: the boys how to be manly, the girls how to be womanly. Men often take over the teaching of boys entirely as the boys grow up, while ignoring further education of girls. For thousands of years, the education of girls has been almost entirely domestic and female, and still is in many places. Men teaching girls who are not their own daughters are mostly a quite re-cent phenomenon. For thousands of years, male priests laid down the laws outside the house; the father of the family enforced them inside the house, teaching little or nothing to the daughters but obedience. The general rule has been that, after age six or so, boys learn from men and girls learn from women, and the more absolute the gender division and hierarchy, the purdah or sharia law, the truer ˙ that is.

By teaching only male knowledge only to boys over a certain age, men have left women the major role in teaching young children the manners and morals of their people – how to be human without reference to their sex. And here lies, perhaps, a fertile ground for change, even for subversion.

The teaching of the fathers tends to maintain hierarchy and uphold the status quo. Social and moral change may begin with women, who have less invested in the hierarchy, as they try to teach their kids how to adapt to new circumstances. I think of the covered wagons on the Oregon Trail; while the men filled the traditional role of aggressively defending their women from strangers assumed to be hostile and dangerous, the women, often surreptitiously, it appears, talked with Indian women, bartered a little with them, left the kids free to nose around one another . . . The rigid white male story excluded the strangers; the opportunistic white female story began to admit them.

A vast amount of what we learn, we learn as story. We hear and read and learn the myths and histories that tell us who we are and who we belong to – the fireside tales that tell us about our immediate people, our family – the official histories of our tribe or nation.

Who tells those stories, who do we learn them from?

Over the centuries, it's been the women of the family who kept alive the stories of who our family is and how members of the family, our immediate tribe, behave. Male priests, shamans, leaders, chiefs and professors taught the stories of who we are and how we should behave as members of our larger tribe, our people, our nation. Women transmit the individual stories, men transmit the public history.

Again, the men's teaching is likely to support the status quo, while the women's teaching, being individualistic, is more likely to be subversive.

The two teachings can be contradictory.

For example, the public, male story I learned of How the West Was Won was about men exploring, leading wagon trains, leading cattle drives, hunting and killing animals, hunting and killing Indians. The stories my great-aunt Betsy told me of her early days in the West were different. I remember Betsy's story of driving away from their burning ranch house with everything they owned in a one-horse wagon. Or her story of how her older sister Phoebe, my grandmother, then twelve, looked after her little brothers in the cabin on Steens Mountain during the Indian troubles while their parents made the three-day trip to town for groceries. The Indians, displaced and harried by government troops, were hostile, and Phoebe was afraid of them, but in the version of the story I remember, nobody hunted or killed anybody.

The public, male teachings and the private, female teachings may differ, and the differences may be confusing: as when a single mother in the inner city teaches her children the story that society expects them to respect themselves and behave as honest citizens, but what they learn from the young men who are the leaders in the streets, and all too often from teachers and policemen, is that they are characters in a story that allows them only one role – to be addicts and criminals, useless or worse.

Or when a family brings up its sons in a story of living in peace and with mercy, but then a male institution, the

174

army, puts them into a war story, where they are driven to kill and be cruel without remorse.

Or when a mother includes her daughters in a rich tradition of skills such as cooking and housekeeping, but then businessmen and politicians persuade them that in the story of capitalist society such work has no value at all. It is not even called work.

A very frequently repeated story tells us that women, innately unadventurous and conservative, are the great upholders of traditional values. Is that true? May it be a story men tell in order to be able to see themselves as the innovators, the movers and shakers, the ones who get to change society's ways, the teachers of what is new and important?

I don't know. I think it's worth thinking about.

THE SECOND EVENING

One of the props that has supported the dominance of men in our society and culture is the idea that great art is made by men, that great literature is by and about men.

When I was in school, women – teachers working, as teachers must, within the male hierarchy – taught me this; and then men taught it to me in college: the really important books are by men, and men are at the centre of the important books.

However, my mother, who was not a feminist, and would disavow any subversive intentions, gave me lots of books by women, including Little Women and Black Beauty, and later on, Pride and Prejudice and A Room of One's Own . . .

When I began to write fantasy and science fiction, that genre of literature really was all about men; very few women wrote it, and its women characters consisted of a princess here and there, a pretty girl screaming in the tentacles of a purple alien, or a pretty girl batting her eyes – 'Oh, Captain, please explain to me how the temporestial figilator works!'

So even though I'd given my heart to several great women writers as well as several great male ones, and welcomed the appearance of actual women characters in science fiction, for a long time I didn't question the idea that fiction was about men, what men did, what men thought. Because I didn't really think about it.

However, along in the 1960s and 1970s those fearsome feminists with their bonfires of bras were thinking and asking questions: Who gets to decide what's important? Why are war and adventure important while housekeeping and child-bearing and child-rearing are not?

By then I had not only written several novels, but kept house for years and had several children, all activities that struck me as fully as important as anything else people did. So I began to think: If I'm a woman, why am I writing books in which men are at the centre and primary, and women are marginal and secondary – as if I were a man?

Because editors expect me to, reviewers expect me to. But what right have they to expect me to be a transvestite?

Have I ever even tried to write as who I am, in my own skin instead of a borrowed tuxedo or jockstrap? Do I know how to write in my own skin, my own clothes?

Well, no. I didn't know how. It took me a while to learn. And it was other women who taught me. The feminist writers of the sixties and seventies. The women authors of older generations, who'd been buried by the masculinist literary establishment and were rediscovered, celebrated, reborn in books like The Norton Anthology of Women Writers. And my fellow fiction writers, mostly younger than I, women writing as women, about women, in defiance of the literary old guard and the genre old guard too. I learned courage from them.

But I didn't and still don't like making a cult of women's knowledge, preening ourselves on knowing things men don't know, women's deep irrational wisdom, women's instinctive knowledge of Nature, and so on. All that all too often merely reinforces the masculinist idea of women as primitive and inferior – women's knowledge as element-ary, primitive, always down below at the dark roots, while men get to cultivate and own the flowers and crops that come up into the light.

But why should women keep talking baby talk while men get to grow up? Why should women *feel* blindly while men get to *think*?

Here is a character in my novel *Tehanu* expressing her belief in gendered knowledge. The central character, Tenar, and her friend Moss, an old, poor, ignorant witch, are discussing male wizards and their power. Tenar asks, What about women's powers? And Moss says:

'Oh, well, dearie, a woman's a different thing altogether. Who knows where a woman begins and ends? Listen, mistress, I have roots, I have roots deeper than this island. Deeper than the sea, older than the raising of the lands. I go back into the dark.' Moss's eyes shone with a weird brightness in their red rims and her voice sang like an instrument. 'I go back into the dark! Before the moon I was. No one knows, no one knows, no one can say what I am, what a woman is, a woman of power, a woman's power, deeper than the roots of trees, deeper than the roots of islands, older than the Making, older than the moon. Who dares ask questions of the dark? Who'll ask the dark its name?'

Over and over, women are heard and read by both men and women as saying what is expected of them, even while saying just the opposite. That speech has been quoted a hundred times by people approving it, endorsing it. Never I have seen a reader or critic pay attention to what Tenar answers.

'Who'll ask the dark its name?' says Moss – a grand rhetorical question.

But Tenar answers it. She says, 'I will.' And she adds, 'I lived long enough in the dark.'

Moss is saying what a masculinist society wants to hear women say. She's proudly claiming the only territory men leave to women, the primitive, the mysterious, the dark. And Tenar is refusing to be limited to that. She lays claim to reason, knowledge, thought, she claims not only the dark but also the daylight as her own.

Tenar speaks for me in that passage. We've lived long enough in the dark. We have an equal right to daylight, an equal right to learn and teach reason, science, art, and all the rest. Women, come on up out of the basement and the kitchen and the kids' room; this whole house is our house. And men, it's time you learned to live in that dark basement that you seem to be so afraid of, and the kitchen and the kids' room too. And when you've done that, come on, let's talk, all of us, around the hearth, in the living room of our shared house. We have a lot to tell each other, a lot to learn.

DISAPPEARING
GRANDMOTHERS
(2011)

I, the High Priestess
I, Enheduanna

There I raised the ritual basket
There I sang the shout of joy

But that man cast me among the dead
> —Enheduanna, *ca.*2300 BCE translated from the Sumerian
> by Betty De Shong Meador

W hat happens to the women?
   I've been writing about it for decades now:
   the masculine orientation of discussion of
books and authors in the press.

Literature is now taught at least as often by women as by
men (though the percentage of women professors drops
as the prestige of the position and the institution rises),
and feminist theory has played a strong part in shaping
recent literary thinking and curricula – but all that is, literally, academic. To the leaders of critical opinion, to the
establishers of rank and value for the general public, to the
canoneers, male value and male achievement remain both
the standard and the norm. Which means that the canon
of literature remains persistently, inflexibly, though now

more subtly exclusive of women.

I'm aware of four common techniques or devices (often, though not always, employed quite unconsciously) for excluding women's fiction from the literary canon book by book, author by author. These devices are denigration, omission, exception, and disappearance. Their cumulative effect is the continuing marginalisation of women's writing.

DENIGRATION

Once bald and forthright, denigration of women's writing now seldom comes right out as misogyny. Only imitators of the flaunting masculinist mystique of Hemingway and Mailer still treat all women's writing as second-rate, beneath notice. But assumptions can be made without being stated.

I don't know of a reviewer these days who would drag out Johnson's comparison of a woman writing (preaching, actually) with a dog walking on its hind legs, or shriek with Hawthorne at the thought of an army of scribbling women grimly advancing on him. The prejudice goes unspoken, the bias is shown by omission. Critics can dismiss whole genres unread if they are associated with women. If mysteries or war novels were brushed off as contemptuously as romance commonly is, or if a male-centred genre got a label as contemptuous as 'chick lit', there would be indignant protest. Many women call certain types of macho writing 'prick lit', but I haven't seen the term used in criticism yet.

A patronisingly jocular tone often serves to denigrate the woman author. Women's writing may be called charming, elegant, poignant, sensitive, but is very seldom called powerful or rugged or masterful. The fact of an author's gender seems to dominate the journalistic mind, gender being read as sexual attractiveness. It's rare to find any discussion of George Eliot that doesn't mention that she was 'plain'. The New York Times obituary of Colleen McCullough, author of The Thorn Birds, included the same tasteful and relevant information. Live or dead, male authors are discussed without mentioning that they are or were ugly or unattractive men, but the sin of not having a pretty face is held against women even when they're dead.

Comparing a book written by a woman to work by other women but not to work by men is a subtle and effective form of denigration. It allows the reviewer never to say a woman's book is better than a man's, and helps keep women's achievement safely out of the mainstream, off in the hen coop.

OMISSION

Periodicals almost universally review more books by men than by women, at more length.

Women's books are reviewed by either men or women, but men's books are reviewed very much more often by men.

Books by women are often grouped together in a joint review, while men's books are reviewed individually.

The most outstanding technique of omission is, as you might expect, in the most directly competitive field: literary prizes. Prize juries commonly shortlist books by both men and women, but give the award to a man.

Except for a prize limited to women authors, I have never seen a shortlist for any literary prize consisting only of women. I was on a jury once which unanimously picked a shortlist of four women. Another juror, a woman, persuaded us that we had to bump one of the women and include a man, or we would be accused of prejudice and our prize would 'lack credibility'. I am very sorry that we let her persuade us.

Shortlists consisting only of men used to be taken for granted, but are now rarer, since they too may be accused of prejudice. To prevent protest, some women are included on the list. The prize, however, will go to one of the men, from two times out of three to nine times out of ten, depending on the prize.

Anthologies tend to show the same gender imbalance. A science-fiction anthology recently published in England contained no stories by women. A fuss was made. The men responsible for the selection apologised by saying they had invited a woman to contribute but it didn't work out, and then they just somehow didn't notice that all the stories were by men. Ever so sorry about that.

'Somehow' one feels that if all the stories had been by women, they would have noticed.

EXCEPTION

A novel by a man is very seldom discussed with any reference to the author's gender. A novel by a woman is very frequently discussed with reference to her gender. The norm is male. The woman is an exception to the norm, from which she is excluded.

Exception and exclusion are practised both in criticism and in reviewing. A critic forced to admit that, say, Virginia Woolf is a great English novelist may take pains to show her as an exception – a wonderful fluke. Techniques of exception and exclusion are manifold. The woman writer is found not to be in the 'mainstream' of English novels; her writing is 'unique' but has no influence on later writers; she is the object of a 'cult'; she is a (charming, elegant, poignant, sensitive) fragile hothouse flower that should not be seen as competing with the (rugged, powerful, masterful) vigour of the male novelist.

Joyce was almost instantly canonised; Woolf was either excluded from the canon or admitted grudgingly and with reservations for decades. It is quite arguable that *To the Lighthouse*, with its subtle and effective narrative techniques and devices, has been far more influential on later novel-writing than *Ulysses*, which is a monumental dead end. Joyce, choosing 'silence, exile, cunning,' led a sheltered life, taking responsibility for nothing but his own writing and career. Woolf led a fully engaged life in her own country in an extraordinary circle of intellectually, sexually and politically active people; and she knew, read, reviewed and published other authors all her grown life. Joyce is the fragile person, Woolf the tough one; Joyce is the cult object and the fluke, Woolf the continuously fertile influence, central to the twentieth-century novel.

But centrality is the last thing accorded a woman by the canoneers. Women must be left on the margins.

Even when a woman novelist is admitted to be a first-rate artist, the techniques of exclusion still operate. Jane Austen is vastly admired, yet she is less often considered as an exemplar than as unique, inimitable − a wonderful fluke. She cannot be disappeared; but she is not fully included.

Denigration, omission and exception during a writer's lifetime are preparations for her disappearance after her death.

DISAPPEARANCE

I use the word in its active, Argentine sense and in full awareness of its connotations.

Of all the crass or subtle techniques used to diminish

women's writing, disappearance is the most effective. Once she is silent and powerless, male solidarity quickly closes ranks against the outsider. Female solidarity or the instinct of justice is rarely strong enough to force the ranks back open, and if the effort succeeds, it must continue endlessly, for the male ranks keep effortlessly reclosing.

I have written before of instances of disappearance that particularly gall me: Elizabeth Gaskell and Margaret Oliphant. Both even now are often referred to only as 'Mrs', the title indicating their gender and their social condition. (We do not refer to 'Mr Dickens' or 'Mr Trollope'.) Gaskell and Oliphant were well known, popular, respected, and taken seriously while they lived. When they died, they were promptly disappeared. Gaskell's work was reduced to the 'sweet' *Cranford*. Social historians of the Victorian era kept reading her novels as documentation, as they read Dickens, but this did not count among the literary canoneers. Oliphant's work was wholly forgotten but for one novel, *Miss Marjoribanks*, not her best, mentioned by historians of literature but not kept in print.

The injustice of these dismissals is as painful as their wastefulness. There really weren't so many excellent Victorian novelists that we can afford to throw out two of them simply because they weren't men. Yet what other reason can be given for the disappearance of their novels? Gaskell is now fairly well reinstated, thanks to feminists and film; Oliphant is not. Why? She and Trollope have a good many similarities; their limitations are obvious, but not fatal; both wrote solidly entertaining novels, psychologically canny and perceptive, which are also fascinating social documents. But only hers vanished. Changing styles put Trollope out of fashion, but he had a great revival during the Second World War when Britons homesick for the old imaginary certainties found them in his books. Nobody remembered or revived Oliphant until the 1970s, when female solidarity in the form of feminist criticism and publishers rescued some of her books at least temporarily.

The rawest case I know of actively disappearing a woman writer is Wallace Stegner's treatment of Mary Hallock Foote. He took the setting, characters, and story of his novel *Angle of Repose* from her autobiography, which was published as *A Victorian Gentlewoman in the Far West*. Even his title is taken from a sentence in her book.

Stegner degraded the character of the author he stole from, making her into an adulterous wife whose careless-ness kills her child – a cruel travesty of the actual relation-ships recounted in the autobiography, the manner of the daughter's death, the depth of the mother's grief. Through-out, Stegner coarsened and cheapened Foote's perceptions of people and landscapes.

Nowhere did he mention Foote or her book's title, de-liberately hiding the fact that she was a published author. The only hint he gave of his source was a sentence in the acknowledgments thanking some friends of his, descend-ants of Foote, 'for the loan of their grandmother.'

Grandmothers are much easier to handle than women who write. Grandmothers don't even have names.

Of course artists borrow constantly from one another, but what Stegner did was not borrowing, it was expro-priation. I would call it plagiarism. It is clear that to him Foote's book simply did not exist in its own right. It was mere raw material for him, the man, the admired novelist, the Stanford professor, to use as he chose. To him, Foote herself did not exist. She was an object for his use.

Rob the grave, just don't say who you left buried in it.

Many who have read Mary Foote's book think it better than Stegner's. Her story was based, selectively, on events of her own life, recounted with emotional control and accuracy. She drew her pioneers and engineers and the Western landscape from life, not second-hand. Stegner sensationalised and conventionalised the setting, the emotions, and the characters. But he was a famous male writer playing the part of famous male writer to the hilt. It worked. He got a Pulitzer for it. His book continues to be printed, praised and studied.

Mary Foote was a woman writer with a moderate popular reputation and no pretension to fame. Her book disappeared. Was disappeared. Though women's solidarity during the second wave of feminism was enough to get it reprinted after a century of neglect, who knows about it? Who reads it? Who teaches it?

Who will think it matters?

I'm thinking now of a woman writer who died not long ago, one who is, I fear, particularly vulnerable to being disappeared: a singularly original and powerful storyteller and poet, Grace Paley. The problem with Paley is that she was – truly and genuinely – unique. Not a 'fluke', certainly, but like so many women writers, she was not part of any major recognised school or trend in fiction or poetry acknowledged by the male-centred literary establishment.

And unlike so many men writers, she was not much interested in the advancement of her ego. She was ambitious, all right, fiercely so, but her ambition was to further social justice in her time.

I fear that if women critics, feminist writers, fair-minded scholars and teachers and lovers of literature, do not make a conscious and consistent effort to keep Paley's work visible, studied, taught, read, and reprinted, it will be quietly brushed aside within the next few years. It will lapse out of print. It will be forgotten, while the work of lesser writers will be kept alive simply because they were men.

It won't do. We really can't go on letting good writers be disappeared and buried because they weren't men, while writers who should be left to rot in peace are endlessly resurrected, the zombies of criticism and curriculum, because they weren't women.

I'm no beauty, but don't give me a headstone that says She Was Plain. I am a grandmother, but don't give me a headstone that says Somebody's Grandmother. If I have a headstone, I want my name on it. But far more than that, I want my name on books that are judged not by the gender of the writer but by the quality of the writing and the value of the work.

LEARNING TO WRITE
SCIENCE FICTION FROM
VIRGINIA WOOLF
(2011)

Published in the Guardian, April 2011

You can't write science fiction well if you haven't read it, though not all who try to write it know this. But nor can you write it well if you haven't read anything else. Genre is a rich dialect, in which you can say certain things in a particularly satisfying way, but if it gives up connection with the general literary language, it becomes a jargon meaningful only to an in-group. Useful models may be found quite outside the genre. I learned a lot from reading the ever-subversive Virginia Woolf.

I was seventeen when I read *Orlando*. It was half revelation, half confusion to me at that age, but one thing was clear: that she imagined a society vastly different from our own, an exotic world, and brought it dramatically alive. I'm thinking of the Elizabethan scenes, the winter when the Thames froze over. Reading, I was there, saw the bonfires blazing in the ice, felt the marvellous strangeness of that moment five hundred years ago – the authentic thrill of being taken *absolutely elsewhere*.

How did she do it? By precise, specific descriptive details, not heaped up and not explained: a vivid, telling imagery, highly selected, encouraging the reader's imagination to fill out the picture and see it luminous, complete.

In her novel *Flush*, Woolf gets inside a dog's mind, that is, a nonhuman brain, an alien mentality – very science-fictional if you look at it that way. Again what I learned was the power of accurate, vivid, highly selected detail. I imagine Woolf looking down at her dog asleep beside the ratty armchair she wrote in and thinking *what are your dreams?* and listening . . . sniffing the wind . . . after the rabbit, out on the hills, in the dog's timeless world.

Useful stuff, for those who like to see through eyes other than our own.

FOREWORD TO
MURRAY BOOKCHIN'S
THE NEXT REVOLUTION
(2015)

'The Left', a meaningful term ever since the French Revolution, took on wider significance with the rise of socialism, anarchism and communism. The Russian revolution installed a government entirely leftist in conception; leftist and rightist movements tore Spain apart; democratic parties in Europe and North America arrayed themselves between the two poles; liberal cartoonists portrayed the opposition as a fat plutocrat with a cigar, while reactionaries in the United States demonised 'commie leftists' from the 1930s through the Cold War. The left/right opposition, though often an oversimplification, for two centuries was broadly useful as a description and a reminder of dynamic balance.

In the twenty-first century we go on using the terms, but what is left of the Left? The failure of state communism, the quiet entrenchment of a degree of socialism in democratic governments and the relentless rightward movement of politics driven by corporate capitalism have made much progressive thinking seem antiquated, or redundant, or illusory. The Left is marginalised in its thought, fragmented in its goals, unconfident of its ability to unite. In America particularly, the drift to the right has been so strong that mere liberalism is now the terrorist bogey that anarchism or socialism used to be, and reactionaries are now called 'moderates'.

So, in a country that has all but shut its left eye and is trying to use only its right hand, where does an ambidextrous, binocular Old Rad like Murray Bookchin fit?

I think he'll find his readers. A lot of people are seeking consistent, constructive thinking on which to base action – a frustrating search. Theoretical approaches that seem promising turn out, like the Libertarian Party, to be Ayn Rand in drag; immediate and effective solutions to a problem turn out, like the Occupy movement, to lack structure and stamina for the long run. Young people, people this society blatantly short-changes and betrays, are looking for intelligent, realistic, long-term thinking: not another ranting ideology, but a practical working hypothesis, a methodology of how to regain control of where we're going. Achieving that control will require a revolution as powerful, as deeply affecting society as a whole, as the force it wants to harness.

Murray Bookchin was an expert in nonviolent revolution. He thought about radical social changes, planned and unplanned, and how best to prepare for them, all his life. This book carries his thinking on past his own life into the threatening future we face.

Impatient, idealistic readers may find him uncomfortably tough-minded. He's unwilling to leap over reality to dreams of happy endings, unsympathetic to mere transgression pretending to be political action: 'A "politics" of disorder or "creative chaos", or a naïve practice of "taking over the streets" (usually little more than a street festival), regresses participants to the behaviour of a juvenile herd.' That applies more to the Summer of Love, certainly, than to the Occupy movement, yet it is a permanently cogent warning. But Bookchin is no grim puritan. I first read him as an anarchist, probably the most eloquent and thoughtful one of his generation, and in moving away from anarchism he hasn't lost his sense of the joy of freedom. He doesn't want to see that joy, that freedom, come crashing down, yet again, among the ruins of its own euphoric irresponsibility.

What all political and social thinking has finally been forced to face is, of course, the irreversible degradation of the environment by unrestrained industrial capitalism: the enormous fact of which science has been trying for fifty years to convince us, while technology provided us ever greater distractions from it. Every benefit industrialism and capitalism have brought us, every wonderful advance in knowledge and health and communication and comfort, casts the same fatal shadow. All we have, we have taken from the earth; and, taking with ever-increasing speed and greed, we now return little but what is sterile or poisoned. Yet we can't stop the process. A capitalist economy, by definition, lives by growth; as he observes: 'For capitalism to desist from its mindless expansion would be for it to commit social suicide.' We have, essentially, chosen cancer as the model of our social system.

Capitalism's grow-or-die imperative stands radically at odds with ecology's imperative of interdependence and limit. The two imperatives can no longer coexist with each other; nor can any society founded on the myth that they can be reconciled hope to survive. Either we will establish an ecological society or society will go under for everyone, irrespective of his or her status.

Murray Bookchin spent a lifetime opposing the rapacious ethos of grow-or-die capitalism. The nine essays in this book represent the culmination of that labour: the theoretical underpinning for an egalitarian and directly democratic ecological society, with a practical approach for how

193

to build it. He critiques the failures of past movements for social change, resurrects the promise of direct democracy and, in the last essay in *The Next Revolution*, sketches his hope of how we might turn the environmental crisis into a moment of true choice – a chance to transcend the paralysing hierarchies of gender, race, class, nation, a chance to find a radical cure for the radical evil of our social system. Reading it, I was moved and grateful, as I have so often been in reading Murray Bookchin. He was a true son of the Enlightenment in his respect for clear thought and moral responsibility and in his honest, uncompromising search for a realistic hope.

DANGEROUS PEOPLE
(2019)

Editors' note: 'Dangerous People' is a text within a text in Le Guin's 1985 experimental novel *Always Coming Home*, a fictional text included as one example of the art forms practiced by the Kesh, the novel's central subjects, a people who 'might be going to have lived a long, long time from now in Northern California', as Le Guin writes in her introduction. The original edition contained only Chapter Two, prefaced by a note by Pandora, a feminist archaeologist whose presence acts as a framing device for the multiple texts across a range of forms that are presented as *Always Coming Home*. Chapter Two is part of this experiment in world building through textual artefacts; the new chapters are more re-flexive, exploring the role of fiction and storytelling in construct-ing good relations.

Le Guin subsequently wrote Chapters One and Three, plus all of their footnotes, as her final piece of completed fiction. The complete 'Dangerous People' was then made available as a stand-alone ebook (US only); hence the footnotes usefully restate mat-erial available to readers of *Always Coming Home*. 'Dangerous People' casts a light on the outer novel's exploration of the complexity of mother-daughter relations in matrilineal households, the legacy of toxic masculinity and militarism, and the lived ecology of Northern California. All that Pandora tells us about Dangerous People's author Arravna is that their name translates to 'Wordriver'.

By Arravna
CHAPTER ONE

Nobody knows why the house named Hardcinder stands
by itself on a rise of slaggy basalt, inside the curve of the
other houses of that arm of the town.* Maybe at some time
they enlarged the common place of Telina but left the old
house standing the way it does, sticking out into the common; or maybe some hard-headed people built the house
there on the common because they wanted a foundation
of rock. Nobody knows now. What happened a long time
ago, or even not long ago at all, even what happens now, is
a matter of memories and inventions and mostly has to be
taken on somebody's word.

So I give you my word:† a good many years ago‡ a
family§ was living upstairs in Hardcinder House, in the five
southeast rooms with the deep balcony that goes around
the corner of the house. The railing of the balcony is carved
with grape stakes and grape vines and goats kneeling and
standing up to eat the grapes. The children who grew up
there knew each wooden goat, the grinning billy, the star-

* Kesh towns were built on the pattern of the heyiya-if, two spiral
curves with a common centre or Hinge. The Four-House (sacred)
arm consisted of the five heyimas or sacred meeting-places, the
Five-House (secular) arm consisted of dwelling-houses, spaced
out in a curve surrounding a common place or plaza.

There were so many houses in Telina that the secular arm had
become three arms, outer, middle and inner, each curving around
its own plaza.

(Note that lower-case 'house' means a dwelling-house; upper-
case 'House' refers to the Nine Houses into which the Kesh
divided all being.)

The largest and most prosperous town of the central Valley,
lying between the Old Straight Road and the River Na.

ing kid, the dancing nanny with her tongue sticking out, the lopsided goat missing one horn, cracked off maybe by some other child playing there some other time. A little girl◊ who lived in that household, though the grinning goat kept his mouth open because he was hungry for the wooden grapes that hung just out of reach, so she put wild oats and parsley in his wooden mouth. Later on, her little son found the fat flank of the dancing nanny a place of comfort to lean on when he needed comforting, and soon after that, her little daughter tried hard to break the one horn off the one-horned goat so it would come out even, but she couldn't do it. A few years later there was a second daughter waving her legs and reaching her arms out to the goats and the grapes. And a few more years later the children of those two daughters were hauling themselves up to stand by holding on to the wooden leaves, learning how to walk, running about the balcony, feeding the he-goat wild oats and parsley. So Shamsha saw green stuff drooping out of his mouth as she came back from the Oak Society workshop, and said, 'Still hungry, are you, goat?' The goat grinned. Shamsha stood a moment at the railing

† A pun both on the meaning of the phrase and on the author's name, Arravna, River of Words.

‡ A familiar literary evasion, understood to mean that though Hardcinder House is a real house, the characters are fictional and the story is a fiction (possibly with some historical or legendary basis).

§ Marai, household, means any number and any combination of blood kin and married-ins living in one house. The Kesh were matrilocal, and house ownership matrilineal, so a mother or grandmother was likely to be at least nominally the head of the family, responsible for the upkeep of the house and the behaviour of family members.

◊ Shamsha, the grandmother at the time of the story.

197

looking down at the common where her grandchildren and other children were playing, and then went indoors, eager for shade and cool water. It was a hot afternoon in a hot summer.

Nobody was in the house but Shamsha's elder daughter's husband Vavetaiveda, asleep on the front-room window-seat. As she walked across town, Shamsha had imagined lying down on that windowseat where the south wind would flow sweetly over her. She had a long drink of water from the cooler[*] and went on to her own room to lie down, but it was so close and stuffy there that she soon got up, bathed and changed, and went into the kitchen. She was restless, wanting work to do. She was chopping mint and chervil for salad when her younger daughter came into the room. Hwette did not speak. On the oaken counter, beside the board on which her mother was chopping herbs, she laid down a plant of chicory: the root, the tough stalk and leaves, the flower stalk at the top, all the flowers but one closed and that one closing, for it was late in the day and chicory is a morning flower.[†]

'That's too old for salad, soubí!'[‡] said Shamsha. She looked around, but Hwette had already gone through to another room.

---

[*] Water was piped into Kesh town-houses, which had interior flush toilets, sinks, and baths. Drinking water was kept cool in the summer by various devices, often large earthenware storage jars that cooled by evaporation, fitted with a faucet.

[†] Many wildflowers had symbolic meaning to the Kesh; chicory signified pregnancy. There are other significations. Hwette is in the morning of her life. The blue chicory flower will live only when growing untouched; if picked, it closes quickly and dies.

[‡] Sou = daughter, -bí attached to a word expresses affection.

Shamsha went on chopping herbs, and put on a pot of cracked wheat to boil so it would be cool by dinner time, continuing to think about what concerned her. She had been for some years archivist of the Madrone Lodge,[§] and last winter in the course of going through old gifts and holdings of the archives had become interested in a manuscript, unsigned, probably written a couple of lifetimes ago, called Controlling. It dealt with aspects of human behaviour that interested her, and people of the Madrone and Oak[◊] had agreed with her that it was a work of originality and insight, worth saving for a while.[¶] She had been copying and editing it since before the Moon Dancing,[*]

[§] Members of the Madrone Lodge undertook to keep records and archives and write chronicles and history either locally or for the Kesh people as a whole (in the latter case they worked at least part of the time in the Madrone Lodge Archives of Wakwaha). Because it dealt with the past, rather than with actuality, the Lodge was considered to belong to the Houses of the Sky. Any person 'living in the Sky House' was considered, to that extent, a 'dangerous' person.

[◊] Shamsha is also a member of the Oak Society, in the Third House of Earth (Serpentine), made up of people interested in literature, written and oral. Closely connected to both the Madrone Lodge and the Oak Society was the Book Art, specifically concerned with the manufacture of paper, ink, paints, the tools of writing, printing, and visual arts, and books of all kinds.

[¶] Concerning the Kesh attitude towards the preservation of documents, etc., see 'Pandora Converses with the Archivist of the Library of the Madrone Lodge at Wakwaha-na', in Ursula K. Le Guin, *Always Coming Home: Author's Expanded Edition* (Library of America), pp. 369-372.

spending several weeks all told at the Exchange[†] to use the writers there,[‡] and today she had been at the Oak workshops talking with people there about using one of the presses and arranging for the paper, for she wanted to hand-set the piece as a book. By the time the Water was danced[§] she would be setting type, but that pleasure would come in its own time. First she must have the text right. That was her concern now. She was thinking about an obscure passage, where the author had missed or miscopied several words through absent-mindedness, or had failed to express the thought in words appropriate to it. She knew how the text might be emended, but not whether she should emend it. Perhaps the obscurity just at this crucial point of the treatise, on which much of the argument hinged,[◊] was deliberate. To offer clarity and withdraw it without warning did not seem characteristic of the author, but it was a complex mind that had thought these thoughts, and the subject, after all, was control.

---

[*] One of the seven annual wakwa hedou, great dances, the Moon was a festival of ritual licence, the most 'dangerous' of all the great dances. It went on for ten nights, beginning at the second full moon after the vernal equinox – mid-Spring. The references place the time of the story as late May or June. See 'Dancing the Moon', Le Guin, *Always Coming Home*, pp. 288-289.

[†] The computer centre at Wakwaha, installed and maintained by the super-terrestrial cybernetic/robotic network known to the Kesh as the City of Mind. See Le Guin, *Always Coming Home*, 'Time and the City', specifically 'Wudun: The Exchanges', pp. 180-183.

[‡] To do research on the computers.

[§] In early or mid-August.

[◊] The noun or verb hinge, íya, is never used lightly; it always hints at further meaning or implication.

So the obscurity might be intentional; or accidental; or non-existent except to Shamsha failing to understand. She was certain only that she must be careful about changing a text which perhaps understood her better than she understood it. So she thought while she carefully rinsed the chopper and the counter, gathered up the bits of stem and wilted leaf, and put them into the compost pail.

All the same, even if the author was deliberately indulging in a compressed allusive mode, the sentence that most troubled her still troubled her. Was it a clear strand across a gap, or a break in the skein, or a knot, a tangle? 'Shattering pressure may induce scattering to find what is traduced.' The chime of *shatter* and *scatter*, *induce* and *traduce*, were much gaudier than this author's usual plain style. Perhaps they signified a sleepy moment, copying out late at night, the mind not in control of the hand, picking up rhymes not reasons. The cracked wheat was done; she stirred it up and left the pot half-open on the stove to cool. Turning back to the counter, thinking of that word *traduce*, she saw the plant of chicory; today's flower now withered shut and tomorrow's buds on the stem mere knots, their promise lost. She felt a little annoyance in Hwette's childishness in forcing her to decide what to do with this small, ungainly, and inappropriate gift. Was she to put it in water root and all? Or to dry the one gangling root to roast for chicory tea? To chop the whole thing up for a bitter note in the salad was the only thing that made any sense at all. But the colour of the closed flower, the blue-violet colour it would be if it were open, was clear in her mind, and in that colour the daughter's gift of that flower to the mother spoke itself, and she understood.

Shamsha stood looking at the chicory plant, her arms apart and still, and then went hurrying down the hall to Hwette's room, saying her daughter's name. But nobody was in the room, or any of the rooms, except in the front room where her son-in-law was still stretched out in the windowseat, looking soft and moist and breathing through his lips so he made a little noise, like a distant engine with a bad valve, puh . . . puh . . . puh . . . Often at night, too, Tai snored in reverse that way. Shamsha's room was next to his and Fefinum's, and once she heard the sound when seeking sleep there was no use trying to think of anything else.

She hurried noisily through the room now, hoping to disturb him, and out onto the balcony. The air that had come hot all day from the east was beginning to come cooler from the south, though still not very cool. Shamsha sat down in a legless wicker chair behind the wooden goats and vines and looked through them over the common place and across the Valley to the hills south of Odoun.* She stretched out her legs and stared at the blue-violet hills. Several times she spoke aloud, saying 'How–' or 'No', or made a small, wordless sound, in the busy distress of her thinking.

Her son-in-law, Hwette's husband,† Kamedan, came up the outside stairs onto the balcony. He said in his low, gentle voice, 'So you're here, amabí.'‡ She looked at him from clear across the Valley. At last she started a little and said, 'Kamedan! Have you seen Hwette?'

'Not since this morning. I've been at the looms,' he said. He stood there, hesitant. Kamedan was a tall, well-made man with dark skin, long hair and clear eyes. He

---

* The town of Chúmo [the setting for the main narrative in *Always Coming Home*] is in these hills.

† Souv giyouda, daughter's husband, so called having formally married Hwette at the Wedding ceremonies of the World Dance.

‡ Han es im, the usual Kesh hello; amabí, dear grandmother.

was strong and beautiful in limb and feature. His mother-in-law looked at him now admiringly and with rancour. She thought: He doesn't know. He won't know till she tells him. She told me first, as she ought. Hwette always does right, always does as she ought to do. The thought was complacent and yet heavy, as if it held other thoughts folded inside it. She put it away from her. She said, 'She was here, and then I lost her.'

Kamedan said, 'I think she was going to the heyimas[§] this afternoon with Fefinum, to Clown practice.'[◊]

'Oh yes, that's right,' Shamsha said, getting up. She found it hard to get up gracefully from a legless chair, but Kamedan's beauty made her wish to be graceful in his eyes. 'All the same, she was here for a minute,' she said, and so saying, thought about the chicory plant. She did not want anybody else seeing it lying wilting on the counter. She went in the kitchen. Tai was there, still moist and creased, but awake, standing up, and breathing through his nose. She did not see the chicory plant. He had spread out a litter of vegetables and implements all over the counter, being as unable to work in an orderly place as Shamsha was unable to work in a disorderly one.

Kamedan had followed her, and now the children came running in, Fefinum's eight-year-old daughter Bolekash

[§] The physical site of the spiritual center of one's Earth House (maternal clan – in the case of Shamsha and her daughters the Obsidian). The five heyimas of the Five Houses were one arm of the double spiral formed by all Kesh towns; the other arm consisted of the dwelling houses.

[◊] The Obsidian Houses provided the ritual Clowns for several of the great dances. Fefinum and Hwette have joined the Blood Clown Society to learn and perform Clown roles in the women's dances of the Blood Lodge.

and Hwette's little boy Torip. Torip fastened his arms around his grandmother as high up as he could reach, which was just below the hips, and said earnestly, 'Ama! Ama, I'm very hungry, I need to eat!' Kamedan poured them and himself cups of lemonade from the jug in the coolroom, and Shamsha fetched down a great bowl of apricots, the last picking of their five trees* in Dry Creek orchard, and the children filled their hands and mouths. Pottering at the counter, Tai asked, 'Shall I get dinner early?'

'It's still too hot. After sunset, maybe,' Shamsha said.

Bolekash said, 'Come on! We're going to the garden!' and whirled out again. Torip obediently followed her, clutching apricots. Shamsha called after them, 'Keep out of the irrigation system, you two!'

'We will,' Torip called back, sweet as a towhee chirping.

Shamsha said, 'They dammed up the ditches this morning and flooded the salad beds. A pair of wild pigs! The wheat's on the stove, cooked, Tai, and I left the herbs in oil, there in the brown bowl. Do you want a hand with

---

* The Kesh idea of property was complicated. Only sacred things were held entirely in common; only one's own body was considered entirely one's own inalienable property. Everything else fell between the extremes. They used the possessive pronouns, but their meaning is often very shadowy, and is a kind of shorthand. Speaking carefully, one would not say 'my family', 'my house', or 'our trees', but 'the people I am related to', 'the house I am living in', 'the trees my family looks after'. The produce of farming and hunting was always shared to a degree determined by complicated traditions and rules. The farm holdings of a Kesh family were usually scattered here and there in a patchwork, cultivated partly by the individual owners and partly as a cooperative enterprise; work and produce were shared according to rule and custom. Shamsha's family may have had various apricot trees in other orchards.

anything else?'

After thinking about it for a while, Tai said, 'No.' Shamsha was relieved. When he cooked, he moved so slowly among such a confusion of implements and unfinished work that it tried her patience, and she often ended up finishing the unfinished for him, which he never seemed to notice. She had already started out the room when he said, 'I guess the peas need to be shelled,' with the air of a person coming slowly upon a concept entirely new to him. Shamsha turned around, picked up the big basket of peas and an empty basket, and went back out on the balcony to shell them.

Kamedan had brought his lemonade out and was sitting there looking out through the goats to the hills. When she sat down with her baskets, he moved closer, took up a handful of peapods, and began shelling, dropping the pods into the empty basket and the peas into his shirt pocket, except for those that went into his mouth.

'Will any of those come back?' Shamsha asked, and he answered, 'Only the ones I don't eat.'

'The book I'm working on describes people like Tai,' she said, 'who by apparently doing nothing cause other people to do things. The author calls it controlling by receding, an important principle, especially useful for controlling people like me. People like me will always come forward as people like Tai recede.'

Kamedan smiled, diffident; he seldom analysed ideas or people. They both shelled steadily. The peas were small, crisp and neat, willingly coming out of their pods under the push of a thumb. They fell musically into the basket in arpeggios as Shamsha shelled and in a pattering rush when Kamedan leaned forward to empty his pocket. His movements were steady and quiet, reflecting his art as a weaver, and his nature, Shamsha thought as she watched him. Yet

205

she did not trust his quietness, his gentleness. It was real but it was blind. Though his eyes were clear, inwardly the man was blind, eyes clinched shut, forehead wrinkled like a bull's, helplessly dangerous.

Shamsha believed that men knew their helplessness, since the rules that bound desire where largely of their making and responding to their needs; but she would like to know a man who did not love his helplessness. She wondered if it has been Hwette's choice to have a second child, or if it was Kamedan's non-choice, his blind doing, the helpless, driven reassertion of potency as paternity, not wanting the child but the fatherhood of the child that bound him to the mother, his emptiness to her fullness.

And why had that child chosen to come to them? Had they yet considered that? Shamsha thought that Hwette might not have considered it and yet, when she did, would be able to answer the question. Hwette had that gift, though she seldom used it. Kamedan, if he considered the question, would not care if he could not answer it. He thought it was enough to welcome the child, to love the child, as he loved Torip. The child was a thread in the fabric of his relationship with Hwette, his marriage the warp on the high, broad loom and he the blind shuttle weaving her life into a pattern, a figure – but really, Shamsha thought, what gaudy metaphors! That book is controlling my mind. Here sits the handsomest man in Telina, shelling peas to help me, thoughtful, careful, kind, the perfect husband for my daughter. Why shouldn't they be having another baby? Kamedan leaned forward to empty a load of peas from his shirt pocket, and the fineness of the corners of his mouth, the innocence of the smile that changed his face from its habitual calm, irresistibly invited her trust and pleasure. Men need marriage, she thought, and it's foolish to begrudge it to them.

Looking down through the goats' legs she saw the two wives, her daughters, coming together across the common from Naward Bridge. Perhaps because her mind was agitated and she had been thinking about marriage, she saw ghosts: her father walked in his granddaughter Fefinum's short, assertive stride, on small feet that turned out a little, planting themselves firmly at each step. And it was the grandmother, Shamsha's mother Wenomal, who turned Hwette's head, lifting the chin, looking up into the evening sky with a bodily gesture so submissive, so remote, that it frightened Shamsha and made her look away, thinking that it is never an altogether happy thing to see the dead, even in the living.

Her two daughters came up the stairs to the balcony, Fefinum talking steadily. Shamsha found herself nervous, feeling ashamed that she had not responded at once to Hwette's message, wanting to make up for that silence now, though she must do so in silence. But Hwette greeted her without the least trace of question or confirmation, so that Shamsha felt foolish trying to catch her eye, and thought she must speak to her later, alone. After Hwette had gone indoors and Kamedan had followed her, Shamsha thought that the best thing would have been to get up and touch Hwette, hold her for a moment; that was all that was needed. But she had not done it. Since her marriage, Hwette had become not easy to touch. Even as a little child, trusting and affectionate, she had been elusive, like the swallow she had been named for then;* and now, like the scrub oak she had named herself for, she was unobtrusive, unwelcoming to the hand.

But, Shamsha thought, whose reluctance am I really

---

* Hwette as a child was called Sehoy, Barnswallow; she renamed herself Hwette, scrub oak, when she was adolescent or grown.

talking about? It was so easy to blame the passive person for one's own active choice, and Shamsha had chosen for a long time, for years now, since Geseta left, not to touch people or be touched unless custom demanded it.

'The child coming to be born demands that the house be set in order,' Shamsha thought, and was afraid.

'Why bother cooking them?' Fefinum said boisterously, scooping a handful of shelled peas from the basket and tossing half the handful into her mouth. She chewed noisily. She was still being a Clown, still enjoying the licence to be crude, loud and greedy, which she thought had been granted her when she joined the Society. That the licence was granted only to the Clown, and that so long as she was Fefinum she was not the Clown, was the kind of distinction that she did not make. Nor did she observe the distinction between her mother the centre of a household, the Archivist of the Madrone Lodge, and her mother, the changing, uncertain woman Shamsha. Fefinum saw the role not the person. Her obtuseness was often very restful to her mother. To be treated like a great rock made Shamsha feel like a great rock. To know her control over people and events was taken as a fact made her feel that she was in fact in control. Fefinum loved control, thrived on it; she couldn't have wanted so badly to be a Clown if she wasn't controlled by control, as the manuscript Controlling put it.

Kamedan came back out on the balcony and took up his place by Shamsha. Fefinum leaned against the curved railing facing the two of them, and stretched out her round, strong legs. She said, 'I want to talk to you two about Hwette.' That was Fefinum practising at being the great rock, the centre of the household. Because the role was more important to her than the person, everything she did seemed like play-acting; and the more important it was, the more dishonest she seemed in doing it. Shamsha felt

Kamedan shift a little, uncomfortable. In herself she felt the ironic and resistant spirit rise, holding its iron flail, ready to strike. I will not speak, I will not speak, I will not destroy her, she vowed to herself.

'I don't think Hwette is ever going to be a Blood Clown,' Fefinum said, low-voiced, tragically important.

Shamsha held her tongue and nodded once.

'She's been coming to Society meetings and learning the dances all summer, ever since the Moon. And of course she does everything right, but I just don't think she has the vocation, the true run of it. And Shaio agrees with me. We talked about it today. Just Shaio and I – not with Hwette, of course. And she agrees with me.'

In Telina the Blood Lodge people call their singer of most authority 'The Eye of the Ewe', and that was what old Shaio was called. The idea of that powerful, stern old woman meekly agreeing with Fefinum, bleating 'oh yes!' like a baa-lamb, made Shamsha say, 'Ah–!' But no more. She controlled herself and kept still.

'But' – Fefinum leaned forward, pointing the fingers of her right hand at Shamsha, all her toes spread out intensely – 'what Hwette has is a much greater calling. I felt that all along. even before she wanted to join the Blood Clowns.'

This was too much for Shamsha. 'She only joined because you nagged her to.'

'I encouraged her. Of course I did. You have to start somewhere, and she was doing nothing, nothing at all.'

'Aside from the house and the gardens and bringing up Torip and helping bring up Bolekash and working at the heyimas, nothing at all,' Shamsha said, letting the ironic spirit flail away. But her daughter's pompous earnestness only increased: 'That's nothing, mother. Nothing to what she could do, what she ought to be. You know that!'

Kamedan said, 'Yes.'

Shamsha drew back into herself, wary as a snail. She set the big basket of shelled peas down off her lap onto the decking. 'What do you mean, ought to be?'

'Shaio says she ought to be learning the great songs. That she has the gift, but isn't giving it.'*

'Then it's hers to give, not yours,' Shamsha said. This time the flail hit. Fefinum winced. Shamsha looked down and shut her eyes in disgust with herself and her daughter. She stood up, picking up the baskets one in each hand, the heavy peas and the empty pods, so that she stood like a scales. 'I don't know,' she said.

Fefinum started to speak again, but Shamsha went on: 'I don't understand spiritual business. I don't go to the deep springs. I'm only an intellectual. But I will say, I think Hwette has enough responsibilities as it is. She hasn't ever been herself entirely since the baby was born–' She stopped short.

Fefinum, no longer play-acting, whether her ambition was for her sister or herself, said quickly but gently, 'That's just it. She's never found out who she needs to be. Isn't it so, Kamedan?'

He said nothing, but nodded once, slightly.

'She's twenty-five years old. With luck she has a considerable length of life in which to find herself,' Shamsha said. 'Don't hurry her. Let it happen.' She went indoors with the baskets, aware that she was running away, evading further confrontation. But how could she talk sensibly about Hwette until she had talked to Hwette about this second pregnancy? And it seemed to her that her last words were not merely conventional wisdom used in

* Gift = badab, give = ambad; the two words in Kesh interplay and interlock to the extent that one implies the other; to have a gift is to give it, the gift is in the giving.

self-defence. In saying them she knew that Hwette did need to be let alone, and that her need was urgent.

She set the baskets down on the counter. Tai was at the stove and didn't turn around. She went to Hwette and Kamedan's room. The curtains were drawn making a warm golden darkness in the room. 'Soubí, soubí', Shamsha said at the door, 'are you in here?' Hwette was sitting on the chest, her hands at her sides. She looked up. In the dusk, Shamsha could not see if she was smiling or weeping or neither. Shamsha sat down on the chest beside her and put her arm around Hwette's round, warm, delicate, vigorous body. They sat still for a while. 'Oh, you, oh, you,' Shamsha whispered, as she had whispered to the new baby daughter. Hwette leaned comfortably against her, fitting into her arm. They were going back to being part of each other. Shamsha drew a deep, long breath. 'Well!' she said, and then nothing more. Nothing needed saying or thinking for a while.

They heard Kamedan's voice outside the window, talking to a neighbour on the northeast balcony.

Shamsha felt tension come into Hwette's body or her own arm. They no longer sat in perfect ease. Words began to press at Shamsha's tongue. She said at last, 'I finally saw the flower, soubí.'

Hwette made a drowsy little uncomprehending sound.

'The chicory flower?'

Hwette stayed wordless and heavy against her. Shamsha wanted to ask a great many questions but said only, 'Thank you for telling me.'

'What chicory flower?' Hwette whispered sleepily.

'This afternoon, soubí,' Shamsha said. The strangeness of Hwette's question came to her slowly, bringing coldness.

'I was thinking about the book, you know, and I was so

211

hot and stupid. The flower lay there before me for I don't know how long before I saw it. It's a wonder I didn't just chop it into the salad without noticing.' Every word she spoke took her further from trust and ease. Every word was true, but when she spoke it it became false.

'Somebody brought you a chicory flower?'

'You did, soubí.'

'I was at the heyimas. With the Blood Clowns. All afternoon.' Hwette sighed and straightened up, leaving the curve of the mother's arm and body. She stretched out her arms into the growing dusk and sighed.

'Hwette, you were here.'

'How could I have been?' She asked the question as if she expected an answer.

Shamsha felt a coldness in the centre of her body. She asked, 'Are you pregnant, Hwette?'

Hwette stood up quickly and lightly. 'I don't know, mamoubí, how can I tell? My bleedings are so irregular I can't worry about them. So if I am I don't know it. Have you been dreaming grandbabies, mamou?' Light as air she moved across the room, gathering up her loose hair and bringing it across her shoulder to braid it.

Shamsha sat cold and confused. 'I don't think I was dreaming,' she said.

Bolekash came running down the hall, calling, 'Dinner is ready, Taibí says!'

Shamsha hurried back to the kitchen and looked over the littered counters and workblocks. There was no chicory plant lying there. But Tai had been working at the counters. She did not want to ask him if he had seen it. His slow mind would seize on the strange question and worry at it and he would talk about it. She'd look in the compost basket after dinner. It might be there. Why hadn't she put it in water or taken it to her own room, done something

212

appropriate with it, the message, the grandmother-word?
Had she really left it lying there along with the parsley
stems and trash? But she had cleaned the counter before
she left the kitchen – she was sure she had. Had the chicory plant been there at all? Had Hwette been there? Was
she asleep on her feet then? Now? She took her place at the
dinner table. 'Thank the food, Bolekash,' she said to her
granddaughter, hearing her own stern voice.

Looking around at what was on the table, the child said,
'Heya! Our praise to you, eggplants, onions, we already
thanked the chicken. Our praise to you, tomatoes, nice
green peas. What's that? Chillies, herbs, rice, lemons, salad, heya hey heya! Shut up, Torip!'

'You didn't thank the pies, you didn't thank the pies!'

'I did too, they're leftovers, I did yesterday.'

'But you ought to–'

'Hush,' the grandmother said, and they hushed, and ate.

In the late, still darkness as the cricket chorus rang like
beaten bells, Shamsha lay awake, thinking that there was a
person she wanted to talk to: Duhe, that Serpentine doctor,* who had been the first to say that Controlling was a
useful book and might not only be kept in the Archives
but copied for use in lodges in the other towns. Duhe was
a person who saw and heard. Shamsha was certain of it,
though they had only talked about the book.

Shamsha had said she intended to take the fragile manuscript up to the exchange to reproduce, to make a sturdy
copy to keep in the Archives; and Duhe – they had been
alone in the Archives reading room – had said, 'Then you

* The Doctors Lodge was under the auspices of the Third House,
the Serpentine, but people of other Houses could join it. Shamsha
is thinking of Duhe as a member of her House, the House of the
undomesticated plants such as wildflowers.

213

don't want to perform it?'*

Shamsha had admitted that she had thought desirous-
ly about hand-copying the text, so as to clarify both the
handwriting and some errors or obscure passages, but
thought this might be mere self-indulgence. 'A doctor
wrote this book,' she said, 'and I'm no doctor, not well
read or practised in this kind of thinking, this healing
thinking. Where I'm in control,' with a glance at the darkened, foxed, spotted manuscript, 'is here in the Archives
alone with the books. That's my learning, my experience.'
Duhe nodded; Shamsha went on, 'Usually I'm a very good
judge of whether an old work is better kept or let go. But
this time, I distrusted myself. This book resonates with my
temperament, my way of thinking, so closely that to me it
was a great discovery, but I don't know if it would mean
so much to other people.'

She had seen in Duhe's face that this confession was
surprising and interesting to the doctor. Indeed, she was
surprised by her own candour and fluency. Duhe listened
in a way that gave one words.

Without exploiting that power, Duhe simply replied
that her opinion was that the book was not only worth re-
producing, but worth performing by hand or even printing, if Shamsha had considered that option.

'Ah! Don't tempt me!' Shamsha replied, laughing, for
there was no work she liked better than setting a text in
type, delighting in the type itself, the ink, the press, the
paper, the first proof, the trimming, the sewing, the binding, in the high redwood workshop of the Oak Lodge,
where the rigorous and demanding mind met the rigorous demands of a material art, and where from that meet-

---

* To the Kesh, a written text was 'performed' by reading it aloud,
or by hand-copying it, or by printing it in letterpress.

ing a book came to be, the most mental of material things. In that place, at that work, Shamsha had known the most intense satisfactions of her life. Not the most enduring, but the purest. Too pure: so that she had avoided the easy obsession, and gone to the Madrone, and become not a maker but an unmaker of books, judging what should be saved and what unmade, the knot of words untied, the letters scattered like seed, the paper gone back to pulp or to earth and ash, to the green shoots and reeds and trees and books of years to come.

'I fed a wooden goat,' she said, and heard her voice thin and weak as a child's, and sat up in bed in the darkness, startled and lost.

What had she been thinking about? About the book, about Duhe, why? Because she wanted to talk to the doctor about Hwette, but that was nonsense, why should she do that? She had been falling asleep. Something had happened which she did not understand, or had not happened. But she was certainly not going to ask a stranger's advice about it. She could run her own household.

Thirty-five years ago Shamsha had joyously married Mehoia. They were living in Wenomal's household in Hardcinder House when their son and daughter were born. Between a night and a morning the young husband had died of heart failure, leaving Shamsha forever distrustful of anything given to her.

Some years later at a dance in Wakwaha she met a man named Geseta, who followed her to Telina and wooed her relentlessly. He was handsome and charming and seemed to Shamsha a great piece of luck, except that he was singleminded. He knew only one story, the love story. To Geseta, life was a means of achieving orgasm. Of course biology was on his side; his sperm and her eggs would agree with him, if they could speak, as would many people of

215

eighteen or nineteen. But there was more to a story than the climax. Shamsha wondered what she was doing in Geseta's love story. But he was so handsome and so accomplished a storyteller that she entered into the plot; she resisted, she wavered, she flirted, she fled, and she succumbed deliciously to his ardour. Their orgasms were many and rewarding.

As his passion waned, he forced it to revive for if living is only one thing the lack of that thing is death. He demanded marriage; he importuned her to the point of harassment. She saw that their story was over, but he insisted on prolonging it past the end. Her resistance became real. Resentful, he called it teasing, provocation. He became jealous, possessive, following her everywhere, but would not talk with her. The anger between them burned high. She set his things out on the balcony.* When he found them, she was alone in the house. He raped her.

To that rape her third child chose to come to be conceived. That was the hinge of the door of Hwette's life.

People would talk, seeing Shamsha pregnant and Geseta gone off to Madidinou; they might well speculate that she had not consented to this pregnancy. Shamsha was chivalrous. Knowing Geseta was unable to endure real shame, she did not tell even her mother that she had been raped. She longed to, but felt that even so much solidarity would

* Divorce was usually by agreement, but a wife could make a one-sided divorce public and final by putting her husband's belongings in a pile on the balcony or outside the ground-level door and telling the other people of the household that he did not live there any more. A man refusing to accept such a divorce would face community disapproval and ostracism. Either party of a marriage could request and usually obtain divorce by putting the matter to arbitration by the Councils of his House.

give her unfair advantage over Geseta, who knowing her strength would founder in his weakness. But it may have been that her strength and his weakness grew in that silence.

To her the rape was one thing and the conception another thing; they were facts of so different a nature that she could connect them only artificially, not in feeling. Justification was irrelevant. What she felt was that this child had chosen to come into her in pain.

The birth was a deliverance, setting free Shamsha's own soul. At Hwette's birth and all through her babyhood, Shamsha knew she had given this child more than she had given the others. They were themselves, but this one was herself given away, set free, not known. She called the baby Sehoy, a common name, but to her holding in it the flight of the swallows at dusk over the River, quick, many, scarcely to be seen, voices veering and disappearing, all but disembodied by swiftness and twilight.

Geseta came back to Telina and fell in love with various women. These days, now that he and Shamsha were getting old, he liked to come around Hardcinder House and indulge in nostalgia, always telling that same old love story though it had become a lie. She did not care if he came or not. Where his passion had touched her was a burn scar, thick and nerveless, an ugly thing but not crippling. Her only feeling towards Geseta was an intense distrust of him with their daughter. Once when Sehoy was four or five Shamsha had found him in the Narrow Gardens with her, picking her honeysuckle flowers to suck. Shamsha had come between him and the child and said to him, 'Never touch her.' Something terrible in her face or voice made him obey. He sometimes made feeble efforts to disobey, to charm and win over the child or to win sympathy for himself in the family, complaining how his heart ached for his daughter and how she was deprived of the simple warmth of his fatherhood by the mother's possessive jealousy. Shamsha ignored all that. But if he made any bodily move towards the child, Shamsha was between them, like a heavy, silent dog with its head and tail down, watching him sidelong.

When Sehoy was grown and had given herself the name Hwette, her begetter laid claim to a superior understanding of her heart and mind, an intuitive link with her. He argued with her against her choice of a name; to call oneself Scrub Oak was self-denigrating, too humble, too scrubby, he said. She should call herself Isitut, Wild Iris: something delicate, beautiful, like herself. When Kamedan began to come to the house, courting Hwette, Geseta talked against him all the time. His jealousy and envy of the young man was so apparent that Shamsha felt a queasy pity for him. He insisted he was only thinking of Hwette's wellbeing. 'Kamedan will destroy her,' he said.

'You should know,' Shamsha said.

'I do know. I know his type. He'll love only one woman all his life. He'll demand everything of her – that she be the world to him, and he the world to her. He'll smother her with love, he'll tie her down with giving. He'll be jealous of anyone and anything that touches her, so he'll keep touching her all over, all the time. She's a wildflower, she can't thrive indoors. She's a hummingbird, like me – needs to move, move. She'll die if she can't go from flower to flower. I used to resent your not letting me touch her, but I see now that you were right; you knew we had to keep hands off her. She's very fragile. She can't take pressures on her, claims on her. Her strength is in her freedom.'

Disgust with his assertion of complicity and distaste for his sentimentality did not quite keep Shamsha from agreeing with him; but she shrugged and said nothing. Hwette and Kamedan were going to marry. And in her beauty of sexual delight, fulfilled desire, pregnancy, motherhood, Hwette was radiant, like a hummingbird indeed, not for fragility but for intensity of life.

Yet that vitality flashed out less and less often. Scarcely at all for how long now, a year? or more? Kamedan was as all-loving of her as Geseta had foretold. He adored her and seemed to depend on her for his being. Neither Mehoia nor Geseta himself had ever drawn from Shamsha, drained her, demanded her as Kamedan did Hwette. It's all very well for a lover to say he'd die without you, but unfair to make it your unremitting responsibility to keep him alive, Shamsha thought. Then she thought, What about Hwette's own life?

The answer was a jolt, a blank. What was Hwette's life?

To Fefinum just now she had said, 'housework, garden work, bringing up her son and niece, working at the heyimas' Well, wasn't that a life, anybody's life? The household, the heyimas; one's family, other people; the obligations and responsibilities, the network of reciprocal and mutual work, observance, care and celebration: what more was there?

A swallow in a net. Kamedan claiming her attention, desire, constant companionship; little Torip and Bolekash needing her attention, care, companionship, teaching; Fefinum demanding that she perfect herself spiritually to fulfil her sister's ambition; and she, Shamsha, the mother, what did she ask of Hwette? To be good, not to bother, be competent, let me get on with my work, my head stuck into the empty spaces between written words all the time. She's the hinge of the household, not I. It all depends on her being here, and she's being pulled to pieces by us all pulling her different ways. She should leave.

Take little Torip and go. Where? To her brother's house in Kastoha, there wouldn't be pressure on her there. Or up to Wakwaha, by herself, leave the child with us, go by herself, go alone, that's what she should do. I'll tell her that, Shamsha thought. First thing tomorrow.

***

Editors' note: Chapter Two of *Dangerous People* appears in the original edition of *Always Coming Home*, prefaced by a note that describes the Kesh practice of writing realist fiction in which spiritual and otherworldly elements are immanent, not fantastical. The note, written in the persona of Pandora, the ethnographer/archaeologist who is researching and reporting on Kesh culture, specifies that Chapter Two has been 'translated for this volume [because it] is exemplary of its kind: the pattern is of two people meeting, or "hinging", or "turning apart", one of whom is then followed to the next meeting with a different person, and so on (the pattern of the heyiya-if repeated) . . . continually deepening the mystery of where Kamedan's wife has "in fact" gone, and with whom, and why.'

Chapter Two begins with Kamedan going to seek medical advice for Torip (Monkeyflower), and ends with Monkeyflower going out to look for his mother. In between, we hear a number of different stories about Hwette's whereabouts before, during and after the action of Chapter One, with the added confusion of the arrival of a company of players, one of whom bears a strong resemblance to Hwette and performs in a play in which she plays a raped and murdered woman, mirroring one implication about Hwette's fate.

But Hwette herself is not present in the chapter – something that Le Guin explicitly redresses in writing the two framing chapters around the hinge of Chapter Two, in which Hwette and her mother Shamsha are the focal characters, placing the story within what could be seen as a feminist awakening around gendered violence and dominance behaviours, so we see political awareness come to a comfortable Valley household.

CHAPTER THREE

If she went up on Spring Mountain dressed in white, the dancers' white, then it could be that she stayed behind when the others left, stayed up on Spring Mountain because she could not bear to go home that night. Her sister Fefinum talked and talked as the dancers went down the path to Telina and she did not want to hear the talk and the talk, so she dropped back, and further back, and stayed to look up at some small birds that were flying away quickly overhead in the sunset light, and then the group of dancers was out of sight down the path, and she stopped walking. After a while maybe she turned around and went back up to the dancing place.

If it was all quiet there and the twilight was coming into the hills and the shadows rising from the low places, from the creek courses and the canyons, then it could be that she sat down in the quietness and let it come into her.

It could be that she went down with the other dancers, hearing their talking, but when they went to the heyimas, she went back to Hardcinder House, and there she left for her mother a plant of chicory, the root and stem, the leaf and flower. As soon as you pick it the chicory flower begins to draw its blue petals together. Before you have it home it has wilted. If she spoke with her mother in the evening of that day, before the household ate dinner, it could be that she left the house again and went back up the path to the place where the Blood Clowns had practised the dances, having it in her mind to dance alone.

If a hunter came through that clearing that evening he would have seen her there.

Each would have been startled by the sight of the other, in that place, at that time. They might have greeted each other, saying so you are here, and then he went on towards the place he liked to spend the night when he was hunting deer. Or he stopped in the clearing and sat down and talked with her, even if she did not want to talk. If it was late dusk when he came to the clearing and he saw only the glimmer of her white clothing, who knows what he thought it was. Maybe it looked to him like the ghost of the woman in the play Tobbe, the ghost of Tobbe's wife who was raped and murdered. Frightened by the ghost, he would be angry at having been frightened. He was a hunter, a man who would not allow himself to be afraid, who would be shamed by fear and angered by shame. He was a dangerous man.

If he frightened her by something he said or did, some movement he made, she might have run from him in panic. He was standing on the way between her and Telina, but there was another path out of the clearing, which met a branch path from Hot Creek and wound on down the foothills to come into Telina from the southwest. It was steep and seldom used, it would be hard to follow in the twilight. On that path she could lose her way and be bewildered. She could fall. If a hunter followed her she could not outrun him and he would certainly catch her on that path.

There would be no use crying out. Those foothills of Spring Mountain are thick-grown with scrub oak and wild lilac and thickets of manzanita, the digger pines stand and fall across the deer-trails, the paths where people may go are few and hard to follow, nobody lives there but trees and thickets, deer and rattlesnake, jay and owl, and all the people of the wilderness.

In Hardcinder House the next morning when they were washing the breakfast dishes Shamsha may have said to her daughter Hwette, 'I think you're tired and anxious, I think you've been dancing too much. Why don't you go and visit your brother in Kastoha for a few days? Leave Torip here, it's time you left him now and then. He needs to learn that he's not the hinge of the universe.'

Hwette would make objections. 'But they want me for the Clown dancing. And Kamedan won't want to go, and he doesn't like me to go away.'

'What difference does it make to him if you're away four or five days? Or a month for that matter? He's well looked after! And he's got his Monkeyflower to dote on.'

'Maybe he'd go with me.'

'The reason to go is to be by yourself. With nobody to look after, and nobody asking you to do anything. Dubukouma and Kodsua are undemanding people, and very fond of you. You can dance with the Clowns in Kastoha if you like. They'd be glad to have you. Just go! You used to go rambling every summer, every fall. Half the year I didn't know where my Swallow had flown to.'

'I was a child.'

'You're that child grown.'

'Woman, not child.'

'Swallow-woman.'

'Scrub oak has roots.'

'Scrub oak is prickly, tough-stemmed stuff that lives on the hard dirt in the wilderness. Nobody put scrub oak in the garden and tends it and says Oh look, how lovely! Oh look, it has an acorn! You need to go over on your wild side, daughter. You need to get out of this house, out of this town. Your roots don't have room enough here!'

Hwette was silent for a while, drying the plates and putting them in the cupboard. Shamsha was about to speak again when her daughter said, 'Maybe I should do as you say.'

If Shamsha was dissatisfied with herself because of the subdued, obedient tone in which Hwette spoke, she could show it only by saying, as she wiped the sink clean, 'Oh I don't know, you should do as you like, only what is it you want, soubí?' and Hwette would not have been able to answer that question. So it may be that she left Telina walking upstream and came to Kastoha-na in the evening of that same day, to the household of her older brother's wife.

***

The copy of *Dangerous People* Pandora sent from the Valley was damaged in transit, and the rest of the third chapter, the last ten or twenty pages of the novel, are lost to us, though not to readers of the Valley of the Na. We can only speculate which of the five places in which she was seen Hwette was actually in that night; and whether Modona killed her and her subsequent appearances were all ghosts, or her 'divided spirit' separated into five, all partly but none fully real. The last possibility seems the likeliest, but we don't know if her part-selves survived this dissolution and rejoined, and if so, whether her marriage with Kamedan was lost or saved. We don't know whether Monkeyflower drowned in the river when he wandered off, or was guided and kept safe by Moondog. If the story has an end, we can only guess what it might be. Kesh stories tend to end with a homecoming, a rejoining, but it is not always a happy one.

224

AFTERWORD

Excerpted from an interview with the author by Arwen Curry, director of the documentary Worlds of Ursula K. Le Guin, *in September* 2011.

Ursula K. Le Guin: Well, this is my study, my office where I write.

Arwen Curry: And when do you usually come in here and work?

Le Guin: After breakfast.

Curry: I imagine you get a lot of emails every day.

Le Guin: Yeah, and it takes a lot of willpower to not do email first. If I have something that I ought to be doing, I'll email till eleven.

Curry: So the important question – where does the cat sit when you're in here?

Le Guin: The cat is usually partly connected to the Time Machine here, and partly to this – this is a gift from a fan. It was just sent to me in the mail. It's a Mobius strip scarf, and as soon as I took it out of the envelope, the cat just laid down on it and started going [growls]. So that's his

Mobius strip and his time machine, and he's very quiet. He just sits there and goes to sleep. Good company. His name is Pardner. He is.

Curry: A cat is a good companion for a writer, seems like.

Le Guin: A lot of writers seem to find it so, yeah. They are quiet. They do, of course, lie on your – well, he's not allowed to lie on my keyboard, but if you put a piece of paper down, the cat lies on it. They're paperweights – kind of nice, friendly, warm, furry paperweights.

Curry: These days, when you come to write, what is it that you're working on?

Le Guin: Well, it would be possibly a poem that I'm revising, working on. You know, poems sort of get chewed over and over and over, and the poem probably started handwritten in a notebook and then got transferred into the computer and then of course the computer. It's only too easy to change words, but then you don't – unless you remember to keep saving another copy, you don't keep the old text. So the computer's not an entirely good place for poetry, but it's so much easier than crossing out and rewriting the poem on another page of the notebook, so it's sort of a battle. Anyway, it might be poetry. It might be something I undertook to write for some magazine or something. It might be a blog. Or it might, I don't know . . . I've always essentially sort of gone to my study to find out what I was gonna write that day. It's still that way.

Curry: You said this yesterday and you also said it in the talk, that you don't think that you're going to write another novel.

Le Guin: I don't think I can. I don't think there's another novel in me. I don't want it to seem I say that lightly, because it is a great loss to me, but on the other hand, I did write a lot of novels and I don't want to write one when I can't do it as well as I used to. I wish I was José Saramago, who wrote a knockout novel at eighty-five, but on the other hand, he started even later than I did, a lot later, so he had to hurry to catch up. But it's sort of a pity, because I do know what I'm doing now and the kinds of writing that I've practiced for all these years, so it's a pity not to use my skill. You know, I've got this craft, so I want to use it on something. So I find what I can do.

Curry: So what is it that a novel requires of you, or what is it that a novel asks of you when you're younger, when you were writing in your forties, let's say? What was that time like? When you were involved in it, what did that mean?

Le Guin: A novel is a large work of art and it requires physical strength to just actually come and do. I mean, I know writing does not use the body very visibly, but there's a great deal of high tension involved, including high blood pressure and a tremendous kind of summoning up of all your mental, spiritual capacities that have gotta be there, sort of on tap.

Composition is hard. I always loved it. I like it better than anything else in the world, I suppose, but I'm not one of these writers that can just sort of sit down and write 5,000 words and that's my day's stint. It was sort of a big deal always, and when it's going well, it's like doing any work you know how to do and you like doing. There's nothing better, but there's always the stops and the breaks and the 'Oh, Lord, is that – now where do I go?' All that.

Anyway, it takes a lot of energy, physical and emotional,

and a lot of staying power, and that stayed with me and in some ways got easier actually in my sixties, when I had fewer other things, the kids grown and gone and people to help me keep the house decent, and there was a freedom. The fifties and sixties were good decades. The forties were tough, because my kids were – my son was still home and life was kind of complicated altogether. But I want to tell people, 'Don't be afraid of getting to fifty, sixty, even seventy. If you got your health and something to live on, they can be really good years.'

permission of the PEN Syndication Fiction Project, and included
in *Searoad* (HarperCollins, 1991).

'The Sound of Your Writing' was first published in
Steering the Craft (Eighth Mountain Press, 1998).

This version of 'Introducing Myself' was written in 1992 as a
performance piece, a slightly revised version was included in
The Wave in the Mind (Shambhala, 2004).

'Off the Page: Loud Cows, A Talk and a Poem about Reading
Aloud' was published in *The Wave in the Mind* (Shambhala, 2004).
'Loud Cows' was first published as the frontispiece of
The Ethnography of Reading (University of California Press, 1994),
ed. Jonathan Boyarin.

'Award and Gender' was given as a talk and a handout at the
Seattle Book Fair in 1999, and first published in
The Wave in the Mind (Shambhala, 2004).

'On Genetic Determinism' was first published in
The Wave in the Mind (Shambhala, 2004).

'Old Body Not Writing' was first published in
The Wave in the Mind (Shambhala, 2004).

'Foreword to Murray Bookchin's *The Next Revolution*' was first
published in Murray Bookchin,
The Next Revolution (Verso, 2015), ed. Debbie Bookchin.

'What It Was Like' was a talk given at a meeting of Oregon
NARAL in January 2004. It was first published in
Words Are My Matter: Writings About Life and Books 2000-2016
(Small Beer Press, 2016).

'What Women Know' was revised from two talks given at the
Winter Fishtrap Gathering in Joseph, Oregon, in 2010, and first
published in *Words Are My Matter* (Small Beer Press, 2016).

'Disappearing Grandmothers' was written in 2011, and first published in *Words Are My Matter* (Small Beer Press, 2016).

'Learning to Write Science Fiction from Virginia Woolf' was first published in the *Guardian* in April 2011, and included in *Words Are My Matter* (Small Beer Press, 2016).

'Dangerous People' was first published in *Always Coming Home: Author's Expanded Edition* (Library of America, 2019).

All above texts are reproduced by permission of the Ursula K. Le Guin Literary Trust.

The Afterword is excerpted from an interview with the author in *Worlds of Ursula K. Le Guin* (2011) directed by Arwen Curry and reproduced by permission of Arwen Curry.

The right of Ursula K. Le Guin to be identified as the author of this work has been asserted in accordance with the Copyright, Designs and Patent Act 1988.

1 2 3 4 5 6 7 8 9 10

Design by Rose Nordin
Typeset in Joanna

Printed and bound in Great Britain by CPI.